MEL BROOKS

Mel Brooks

Disobedient Jew

❖◈❖

JEREMY DAUBER

Yale
UNIVERSITY
PRESS

New Haven and London

Frontispiece: Publicity photograph of Mel Brooks, 1961
(Courtesy of the Billy Rose Theatre Division, New York Public Library)

Jewish Lives® is a registered trademark of the Leon D. Black Foundation.

Yale University Press books may be purchased in quantity for educational,
business, or promotional use. For information, please e-mail sales.press@yale.edu
(U.S. office) or sales@yaleup.co.uk (U.K. office).

Set in Janson Oldstyle type by Integrated Publishing Solutions.
Printed in the United States of America.

ISBN 978-0-300-24427-4 (hardcover : alk. paper)
Library of Congress Control Number: 2022933159
A catalogue record for this book is available from the British Library.

This paper meets the requirements of ANSI/NISO Z39.48-1992
(Permanence of Paper).

10 9 8 7 6 5 4 3 2 1

Jacket photograph © Al Satterwhite

To Miri

For making me laugh, and for laughing

CONTENTS

MEL BROOKS

Introduction

"YOUR OBEDIENT JEW, Mel Brooks," was how he often signed his letters, and in that signature lies the essential contradiction of his nature.[1] The deep-seated need to be loved, accepted, *adopted* by all; and the irresistible, rebellious urge to take the universal, the standard formula, and to make it funny by making it Jewish.

In chronicling Brooks's life—his *Jewish* life, which in his case amounts to almost the same thing—that same ping-ponging between allegiance and rebellion appears over and over again. Observe the tension between an almost slavish devotion to authority, be that authority classic Hollywood film, Sid Caesar, or nineteenth-century Russian literature, and the need to remind that authority that a Jewish eye, and a Jewish tongue, can deflate even the most august of genteel (and gentile) structures. In that way, Mel Brooks, more than any other single figure of

MEL BROOKS

the twentieth century, symbolizes the Jewish perspective on, and contribution to, American mass entertainment.

In that way, and many others. Take, for example, his un-flagging energy, almost—but not quite—a mania, and almost—but not quite—a metaphor, for first-generation American Jewish energy. To witness Mel Brooks, in any of his television appearances or movie roles, is to watch a man incapable of sitting still. He wants to lay waste to the place, to reduce it to ashes in the smoldering fire of his comic genius. But Brooks is no anarchist, no Groucho Marxist: his ultimate decision—following a path so resonant of so many other American Jewish success stories—is that the secret lies in constraining himself within the system, rather than working outside of it.

Sometimes, those constraints appeared in human form. On the talk shows and variety hours where he first made his name, they appeared in the guise of an interviewer/straight man to keep him on track, with Carl Reiner, the first among equals, guiding him through his paces in the 2,000-Year-Old Man routines. In his films, the constraints took the form of either stand-ins—Zero Mostel channeling his id in *The Producers* to Gene Wilder's superego, and then Wilder taking turns as both id *and* superego in *Young Frankenstein*—or scene partners, to balance and bleed off his energy like a safety valve. (Think of Madeline Kahn in *High Anxiety*, or Marty Feldman and Dom DeLuise in *Silent Movie*.) Much of this book will tell the story of Brooks's work through his encounters with partners in comedy and art, Jewish and, on occasion, non-; a roll call of American twentieth-century comedy culture.

But by far Brooks's most important self-constraint was his favored form: the parody. He came by his love honestly; the site of his apprenticeship, Sid Caesar's *Your Show of Shows*, practically reinvented the form for postwar mass entertainment. But Brooks took it further, making the parody nothing less than the

2

essential statement of American Jewish tension between *them* and *us*, culturally speaking; between affection for the mainstream and alienation from it. When Brooks said about making *Blazing Saddles* that he was "trying to use every Western cliché in the book—in the hope that we'll kill them off in the process," he was speaking as the closest possible observer of those clichés, and the sharpest possible critic. You can't be the master parodist of the American Western (and the American horror movie, and the American silent film, and the American suspense picture, and so on) without a deep familiarity and love for the material. And yet you have to be outside it as well: to feel estranged enough from it to point out its flaws, its ridiculous features, its aesthetic omissions and even its moral failures. In short, you have to be the loyal opposition: which is as good a way of describing a certain American Jewish attitude as any.

But Brooks would not be the genius he is if his work didn't raise artistic questions at the highest level: and perhaps his testing of limits, his pushing against constraints, is most powerful and profound when it comes to the questions of suitable or tasteful subjects for comedy itself. It should never be forgotten that Brooks was a major American box-office draw for most of the 1970s, far more financially successful than, say, Woody Allen—and for most of that time, and for most of his audience, those questions revolved around vulgarity. (The flatulence scene in *Blazing Saddles* is the "Here's looking at you, kid" of American low comedy on film.)

But for many others then, and for even more now, Brooks's lifelong engagement with the Holocaust as a source of comedy is substantially more significant. Half a century after *The Producers* first astonished and alienated audiences, the questions Brooks raised about the ethics of Jewish comedy feel more resonant today than ever: with Larry David under fire in 2017 for telling a Holocaust joke in the opening monologue on *Saturday*

Night Live, and the troubling employment of "Holocaust humor" as an alt-right recruitment strategy, Brooks's own ur-Holocaust comedy seems more important to think about than ever.

For someone of Brooks's cultural stature, there are surprisingly few books written about him; and even fewer works dedicated to a sustained treatment of Brooks as a Jewish artist. I hope to correct that omission here, in a biography shaped and focused by particular moments, preoccupations, and sensibilities. And speaking of sensibilities: although the thinking and research that have gone into the book are, of course, serious, no book about Mel Brooks should be *entirely* unfunny. And so befitting its subject, I'll try to throw in plenty of examples and anecdotes to illustrate one of the most colorful and dynamic lives in American show business.

"So den, what are you waiting for?" one can hear the master (stage) whispering. "Get to it, already!" And so off we go.

1

A Jew Grows in Brooklyn

IN THE FIRST YEARS of the twentieth century, a Yiddish writer named Avrom Reyzen wrote a gem of a short story—a little comic toss-away—about a man who went searching for America, but he didn't have the money to get very far, so he got as far as Brooklyn, and that's where he stayed.[1] Looking at the bright lights and the rising skyscrapers of the city from across the East River—that dominating poetic symbol of ambition and engineering modernity, Roebling's bridge, spanning the waters—that was where the Jews made their lives, in the borough's brownstones and cobbled streets. Alfred Kazin would walk the streets of the city; Mel Brooks would float slightly above them. Or so he would describe it.

Brooks was *Amerikaner-geboyren*, the native son of two immigrants. It was a mixed marriage, of a sort: Max Kaminsky was part of the German-Jewish wave, emigrating from Danzig as a boy, his father starting a booming herring concern on the Lower

East Side, while his mother, Kate Brookman, was born in Kiev, coming over at the age of two. Max and Kate met in the city, married in 1916, moved to Brooklyn, and proceeded to produce four boys: Irving, Lennie, Bernie, and Melvin, a quartet that sounds straight out of an American Jewish vaudeville punchline. Young Melvin Kaminsky arrived in the world on June 28, 1926, on the family kitchen table (home delivery was common in those days), and was only about two and a half when his father Max, a paralegal, process server, insurance investigator, and public notary, died of that all-too-common Lower East Side ailment, pulmonary tuberculosis, on January 14, 1929. He was thirty-four. This was a second abandonment for Kate, of sorts: her father had deserted his family in 1906, one of the many "disappeared husbands" of the New World, the kind posted on the pages of the *Forverts* with pictures that looked like mug shots—forcing Kitty and some of her siblings to spend part of their childhood in the Hebrew Orphan Asylum in what was then Jewish Harlem.

Though the extended family helped out, the social safety net being what it wasn't, Kitty Kaminsky, along with all three of Brooks's older siblings, were forced to go to work to make ends meet—in the garment trade, as shipping clerks, newspaper sellers, runners. Melvin, of course, was too young to do so, even by the lax child labor standards of the day, with the result that he became—in a familiar dynamic to many Jewish-American families of the time—the babied repository of the family's emotions: loved, loved, loved. "I was adored," he would say later. "I was always in the air, hurled up and kissed and thrown up in the air again. Until I was six, my feet didn't touch the ground. Giving that up was very difficult in life."[2]

Volumes have been written about the role of early familial tragedy in the development of the comedian, the lust for affection and attention, the need to act out and act loud. It's almost impossible to find a purer example of the type than young Melvin, who was talking at sixteen months, *tummeling* with abandon in grade school, and was the undisputed champion of the street corner. With the liberty granted and forced on him by his mother's and siblings' jobs, Brooks took to the streets. ("We didn't have any trees. The good earth to me was cement.") Those Brooklyn streets were a classic training ground for the motor-mouthed Jewish kid, short in stature and long in sass, who'd rather use his wits and feet than his fists but would sometimes have to use all three. "Either you were hearing a joke or repeating a joke," Brooks said; "comedy was born on street corners." Jewish street corner alumni included Joe Ancis, who would teach the art of the fast-paced, free-flow, wild-man *shpritz* to Lenny Bruce, and Jack Kirby, who'd pugnaciously shape the four-color collective imagination in comics for decades to come.

"We grew up on those stoops," Brooks would say. "We played stoopball. We'd spread the Jewish newspapers, the *Daily Forward*, which was like the Jewish *New York Times*, or the more progressive *Freiheit*."[3] Yiddish, in other words, was pervasive, literally underfoot. Along, of course, with its speakers. "I thought Christians were a minority, I really did," Brooks would say, expressing a sensibility, if not an actual belief. "Morning, noon, and night, all I ran into were Jews." Understandably: Brooks's Brooklyn neighborhood of Brownsville was estimated to be 75 percent Jewish the year he was born.[4]

Jewish Brooklyn of the time was also, as Brooks would later put it, "a hotbed of artistic intellectuality," expressed, perhaps most prominently, in theater and music. "Above all they loved theater . . . these tenement Jews loved books and serious plays—Boris Thomashefsky-type plays."[5] Brooks's choice of Tomashevsky isn't surprising; that grand, stalking figure bestrode the Yiddish stage like a colossus. But his preening physical presence, his love for historical drama, his insistence on the model of actor-manager-director-producer: this was more than an example. Knowingly or no, it would serve Brooks as the first of many artistic templates. And that sense, pervasive in the Yiddish theater, that it wasn't *really* a play if it didn't have some music in it, spoke to another future essential component. Music was almost woven into the American Jewish immigrant life—and for ambitious and creative Jews it could provide another entrée into the entertainment business as well, via vaudeville and its cinematic adaptations. As Brooks would recall almost three-quarters of a century later, "Though it was the depths of the Depression, there was music everywhere. Not Vivaldi or Verdi, but the popular music of the day . . . I knew the lyrics of all of 1935's greatest hits and loudly sang them all day long as I happily danced along the sidewalks."[6]

Theater, music, and movies. Like the other Brooklyn-born Jewish comedian-director-auteur who would change his name and grow up to dominate film comedy in the 1970s, Melvin grew up in the grand age of movies, before, as they put it, the pictures got small. Almost a decade older than Allen Stewart Konigsberg (later, better known as Woody Allen), Brooks was old enough to fully inhabit—as a small child—an entertainment world in transition from the silent film to the talkies, Chaplin and Keaton as well as *The Jazz Singer.* "This was much better than real life," Brooks said, about the movies. "Who needs real life?"[7] It would not have escaped the family notice that the first commercially successful "talkie," released when Melvin was a year old, was deeply connected with Jewishness; the titular Jazz Singer's attempt to balance the desires and siren song of modern entertainment with fidelity to Jewish identity and tradition was also making it clear, from the very beginning, that the voice of film was, or at least could be, a Jewish voice. It was a lesson Melvin would take to heart.

Of course, even precocious as he was, Melvin was too young to appreciate *The Jazz Singer* in its original release; but he did see a Hitchcock film, *The Lodger,* at six (he remembered watching it as "a little kid in Brooklyn, eating knishes") and *Franken-*

stein, that classic Universal horror film, even before that.[8] (It gave him nightmares that the monster was climbing up his fire escape.) Was it cheap babysitting, a way of keeping out of trouble? (Brooks would sometimes stay at "some dump neighborhood theater" from opening at 11:30 in the morning till night.) Was it that the notions of family viewing were different then, that mass entertainment was less differentiated by age than it is today? Regardless, Melvin went to the movies religiously, Saturdays at the Marcy Theatre—he loved Westerns particularly, but also the hijinks of the Brothers Marx and Ritz (the latter, who came from the neighborhood, featured a singing and dancing Frankenstein as one of "The Horror Boys from Hollywood" in 1936), and, perhaps most of all, 1930s musical comedies like the Fred Astaire–Ginger Rogers movie *Swing Time*, from that same year, which he'd later call his favorite movie.

And the outer-borough kid dreamed of the Great White Way, which was everything Manhattan was supposed to be: sophisticated, cosmopolitan, rich, and, of course, more than ever so slightly Gentile—the kind of club that probably wouldn't have wanted him for a member.[9] "When we were kids," Brooks would say later, "we'd walk across the Williamsburg Bridge to the Lower East Side and that was okay, there were a lot of Jews there. However, when we'd go any farther uptown it became very scary and very exciting at the same time."[10] Reinforcing the point was a first visit to Broadway at nine with his Uncle Joe ("a philosopher, very deep, very serious . . . 'don't buy a cardboard belt,' he'd say"), a day that, Brooks recalled, "infected me with the virus of the theater." The show was Cole Porter's *Anything Goes*, and the lead was Ethel Merman: a combination of British gentility and sheer, belting, outer-borough moxie (although the Queens-born Merman hailed from Presbyterian and Episcopal, not Jewish, roots). What's more, the show's title song could have served as an *ars poetica* for the future auteur of liberation from constraint: what was once shocking in olden days is no

9

longer apropos—these days, anything goes. Brooks would sing and dance around the point, shifting it subtly, but this musical—and musicals generally—settled deep into his DNA. And, in the process, unearthed a calling. "Way up there at the top of the second balcony, I figured that I was as close to heaven as I'd ever get," he later reminisced. "On the way home, still buzzing with the excitement from the show, I made up my mind . . . I said, 'I am going into show business and nothing will stop me!'"[11] And soon after Melvin's bar mitzvah, when the family moved to Brighton Beach, he found his instrument.

The drums seem a perfect match for the man who would become Mel Brooks: capable of drawing all the attention in the room, making a crash and a bang, but also capable of tight, close rhythm. The drums are also—generally speaking—an instrument that follows the melody, amplifies and backbeats around it, rather than coming up with the melody itself. They are, in some sense, a perfect instrument for a parodist. Not to mention being great for the comic rim shot. They are, far and away, the most popular instrument for comedians to play, Steve Martin's banjo and Woody Allen's clarinet notwithstanding.

Melvin's experience with drum lessons both echoed the tight-knit nature of the American Jewish community, where it seemed everyone knew everyone, and prefigured a career marked by constant proximity to and involvement with the great and the good. A nearby neighbor in Brighton Beach named Buddy Rich, the older brother of Brooks's high school bandmate, offered to give the teenage Brooks drum lessons, and the guy had *yikhus*, a pedigree: he'd played in Artie Shaw's big band, as high a recommendation as you could get. It's not clear that Melvin's musical abilities actually required the masterful talents of one of the most famous drummers of the twentieth century—and it's not clear how often or how long Rich actually taught him—but it sufficed. Enough for him to play weddings and bar mitzvahs under the name "Melvin Brooks," claiming the reason for the shortened version of his mother's original name was that something longer didn't fit on the bass drum (but probably also because he kept getting confused with the jazz musician Max Kaminsky). Enough to help him get the break behind his big break. Many years later, as Brooks told the story, when he made *Blazing Saddles*, Rich embraced him, weeping. "You're going to be a movie director," he said. "So?" Brooks asked, wondering at his tears. "You coulda been a good drummer," Rich replied.[12]

Brooks's career path sometimes seems so perfectly cast it feels more like a metaphor than actual biography: epitomizing the history of American Jewish comedy—American Jewry—in the twentieth century. And, in its own ways, it combines a trail-blazing nature with a sense of belatedness: like the work of all great parodists, it has to follow simultaneously with leading. Brooks was frequently, in the early days, a little too young for the main event, playing to his advantage and creating guilt simultaneously. He plays while his older siblings work. And when the Second World War broke out, he was too young—at least in the war's early years—to enlist. But he started to help earn his share at an early age, and he did so in the most American Jewish manner possible: by going to the mountains.

The Borscht Belt was at its height then, with families flocking to the Catskills to escape the city heat for the week, their working and sweltering fathers riding up to join them on the weekends for heaping portions of food and entertainment. In 1940, the fourteen-year-old Brooks got a job at Sullivan County's Butler Lodge via a Williamsburg acquaintance, the social director of the nearby Avon Lodge. It was mostly menial work, in the kitchen and the boathouse, eight dollars a week plus room and board. For a while, he was assigned—this is not a joke—to the sour cream station.

But on the side, he begins to entertain.

The *tummeler* is an almost impossible phenomenon to fully describe in all its low majesty. "Someone who makes sure that everyone is having fun" makes it sound like a cruise director with a clipboard. "Someone who walks around doing funny things" makes it sound . . . more extraneous to the mountain phenomenon than it was. "Performance artist" is closer, but it omits the sense of the viewer's involvement by virtue of being tummeled. Brooks, of course, has the perfect definition: "a busboy with tinsel in his blood."[13] The tummeler is atmospheric, reminding the hotel guests that they are in a different space, a world in which comedy can bust out at any time. Something, in fact, like the world certain film characters inhabit.

At least this must have been the sense of anyone sitting by the pool of the Butler Lodge in the summer of 1940, who could have seen, on numerous occasions, a young boy, dressed in something that could have been a remarkably ill-fitting black alpaca coat and derby, walk onto the diving board, holding two cardboard suitcases filled with rocks. With a primordial wail, the call of the nebbish—"Business is terrible. I can't go on!"— the young man would drop into the pool, suit, suitcases, and all. The commitment to the bit—to the comedy, to the fact that performance and life were all tied up together in a very serious way—was the fact that Melvin could not swim, and so had to be fished out by lifeguards after each performance. "Look, I had to take chances or it wasn't fun being funny," he'd later say.[14]

But really, would you expect anything less? Brooks had a commitment to painful and dangerous comedy from the first. It gleamed in the first sketch he ever wrote, for a Saturday show at the Butler the following summer. It was a two-hander: Brooks and a young woman. He, claiming he's a masochist, asks her, a self-professed sadist, to hit him. She complies. Brooks's response: "Wait a minute, wait a minute, hold it. I think I'm a sadist."[15] Adept in the language of psychological neurosis, yes; short, snappy, and funny, yes; and also, not insignificantly, requiring Brooks to take a blow every time it's performed. Analysts take note.

But Brooks had not broken through as a performer yet, or a writer, by any means. The summer after *that*, in 1942, he was in show business—but very much in a support capacity. He wasn't a comedian, but thanks to his drum lessons, he was able to sit behind the comedians, provide them with support—rim shots, mostly. Behind, however, was never a position that sat well for too long with Brooks; and one night, when the comic was sick, Mel went on in his place. The first night was a stale retread of the house comic's act; but the second night was magic. The story goes that before the fabled performance, there'd been an episode that set the entire hotel abuzz: Molly the chambermaid had gotten locked in a closet. *"Loz mir aroys!"* ("Let me out!") she shouted, until someone came to her rescue. The next night, that was how young Melvin Kaminsky began his act—with a Yiddish yawp of a demand for self-liberation, to let the harness off—and that was that.[16] The audience was eating out of his hand, and he had learned the power of the contemporaneous, of the ad-lib based on the moment: it's just you've got to repeat it faster and louder. He stayed the house comic for the rest of the season.

But even with Melvin's success, he was of course a minor player, at best, in the starry firmament of the hotel entertainment hierarchy. There were masses of comedic cannon fodder thrown at the constantly starving (in both senses of the word) audience, and when it came to musicians turned comedians, there was no contest: the Avon, not the Butler, was the place to look, where a former saxophonist with a God's-gift of double talk had viewers packed around the porch lights and peering through the windows as he held forth. There was no way that Melvin Kaminsky could hold a candle to Sid Caesar—the man was just born gifted; the strength, the performance chops, the *voice*, even the name, unbelievably, naturally his by birth, the most perfect Gentile performer's name you could imagine— but that wasn't too much of a problem, because *no one* could hold a candle to Caesar. It was like being jealous of the lightning. Years later, Brooks would recall: "Sid was the Apollo of the mountains, the best looking guy since silent movies. He would stretch himself out on a rock near a lake and we'd all stand and look at him."[17] Their paths crossed at the time, briefly, but only as acquaintances, the star and the star-struck.

The idylls of the Borscht Belt, the most Jewish space in America, were—as everyone understood, in their kishkes, with a twisted irony—born of anti-Semitic restriction: they won't let us into *their* hotels, so we'll make our own, with more food and better fun. And everyone understood, also, the furnace of anti-Semitism that powered the Nazi regime in Europe. Like many others in the mountains, and in Eastern District High School (the family had moved once again, in the interim, from Brighton Beach back to Williamsburg), Melvin had extended family in Nazi-occupied Europe; and whatever he and his community knew precisely about the contours of the war against the Jews, they knew it wasn't good. Even closer to home, all of his three brothers were in the service, two of them overseas; his brother Lenny was shot down over Austria in 1944 and held as a POW for the remainder of the war; he'd managed to pass as Polish, since if he'd been identified as Jewish by the Nazis, things might have gone far, far worse for him.[18] Melvin hated Nazis for good reason, and with a passion—an animating hatred that would continue throughout his career—and he enlisted as soon as he turned eighteen, following all his brothers' examples. The same week, Leonard went MIA.

That was June 1944, the month of D-Day; by virtue of his age, Brooks's wartime service was necessarily shorter than many others'. For Brooks, like many other big-city Jews of his era, the army was a formative and sustained encounter with non-Jewish America, and although he claimed to love it—it was where he "learned to eat a cheeseburger" and "dance the waltz with beautiful Southern belles"—it wasn't always pretty.[19] Sent

to the Virginia Military Institute for training in more specialized technical skills thanks to a high score on an Army classifi-
cation test, he was called a "dirty Jew" in the commissary line;
he went for the guy with his mess kit, being a "tough Jew from
Brooklyn."[20] The program he was in at the VMI disbanded,
and Brooks ended up finishing basic training at Fort Sill, Okla-
homa; by the time he did, Paris was already liberated. Which is
not to say he didn't see action.

It shouldn't be forgotten, in all the conversation about
Brooks and Nazis, that he actually fought them. Brooks landed
at Le Havre in February of 1945 and was a forward observer for
the military and part of the 1104th Engineer Combat Group.
He remembered seeing bodies "along the roadside . . . wrapped
up in mattress covers and stacked in a ditch," and ordering the
"old men and little boys" the Germans sent against the Allies at
the war's end to throw down their guns and surrender in a mixture of German and Yiddish.[21] (He also responded to Nazi pro-
paganda announcements by singing "Toot Toot Tootsie" back
at them via bullhorn.)[22] But his main role, particularly after
V-E Day and a promotion to corporal—he was holed up in a
wine cellar near Wiesbaden the day Germany surrendered—
was as a noncom "entertainment specialist" in Special Services,
which were essentially GI tummelers for the American military
still in Germany. Brooks scheduled USO tours and amateur
soldier productions alike for whole divisions, sometimes acting
as master of ceremonies, during which—for the first time, at
least in public—he tried out his Hitler impersonation (and saw
a four-photo spread of himself mugging and pulling faces appear in *Stars and Stripes*).[23] He was nineteen years old.

Brooks finished his hitch Stateside in spring 1946, back in
New Jersey as Fort Dix's head of entertainment, where he and
two friends were most notable for their hairy-legged, unshaven
version of the Andrews Sisters, performing the songs of the
popular wartime trio to delighted audiences. But that wasn't

Melvin Kaminsky's only musical effort. He had his own theme song, which he presented to the audience in that *Jazz Singer* Al Jolson hand-on-heart approach:

> Da-da-da-da-dat-da! Here I am.
> I'm Melvin Brooks!
> I've come to stop the show.
> Just a ham who's minus looks.
> But in your hearts I'll grow!
> I'll tell you gags, I'll sing you songs.
> Just happy little snappy songs that roll along.
> Out of my mind,
> Won't you be kind?
> And please . . . love . . . Melvin . . . Brooooks!

From the perspective of a literary critic—or, for that matter, a psychobiographer—it's all there, isn't it? The need for attention and affection; the concern about personal appearance; the ars manifesto as an ad-libber (the songs roll along "out of my mind"; unless it is simply that *he's* out of his mind); the mixture of music and comedy . . . Brooks, like many of the most successful commercial artists, understood exactly who he was from the very beginning. An essential part of which, of course, was a performer. A man of the theater, who's come to stop the show, and who needs the audience to make up their mind—to change their mind—from their first, perhaps negative impression.

If this reminds you of the plot of *The Producers*, you're getting warm. But Brooks had a way to go in the theater first.

He'd returned to Butler in the summer of 1946, this time as a veteran (in both senses of the word) social director, but that felt like a dead end, out of the spotlight. The next year, after some brief stints as a postal courier and a ladies' wear salesman at the Abilene Blouse and Dress Company, and perhaps a (very little) bit of time in classes—Brooklyn College, which he frequently claimed to attend, has no records of him matriculating—Brooks joined the Red Bank Players, a New Jersey theater group, that summer. His time there would set a pattern repeated on many future occasions, starting in a minor role in the institution, then expanding his ambit: he began as a stagehand, and then, when the director quit near the end of the summer, took over that role, where he blossomed.[24] But New Jersey was still *Jersey*; small time, when city lights beckoned.

Like the ones around the Copacabana, where Caesar was starring in a revue; whether or not it was indeed, as Barry Manilow would later assert, the hottest spot north of Havana, the Copa had plenty of heat. That same summer, 1947, Groucho Marx and Carmen Miranda starred in a movie that shared the nightclub's name. Although the film didn't quite capture the actual club's sizzle (the *Times* reviewer Bosley Crowther suggested it was "furnished with all the usual fixtures of a Hollywood nightclub film—meaning chorus girls, musical numbers, cardboard characters, and an idiotic plot"), its ingredients, mixed differently, became a recipe for significantly more accomplished films later on.[25] Brooks, by contrast, was trying to peddle one-page headshots all over town, even busting into über-producer Kermit Bloomgarden's office under the pretense that he was the Yiddish theater actor turned movie star Paul Muni. When Bloomgarden saw him, he said, "This boy is not Paul Muni." Brooks, not missing a beat, responded, "Muni's name is Harold Gottwald. *I* am the *real* Paul Muni." The joke went around and around, since Muni *had* changed his real name—from Muni Weisenfreund—and, for that matter, Brooks had changed his: emblematic of the period's blurred and constantly refashioning American Jewish identities in the entertainment world. Bloomgarden got the joke, even savored it—"You've got a lot of moxie, kid. I'm going to remember you," Brooks recalled him saying. But it didn't get him a gig.[26]

It was different with Caesar. The Copa headliner, like his Roman namesake, was always someone who enjoyed being worshipped, and Brooks, in the market for a father figure, was someone who was happy to be deeply worshipful. The two renewed their relationship backstage, and with the dynamic set in stone, they became close over après-show hangouts during Caesar's subsequent triumphs at the Roxy and the Broadhurst (1948's *Make Mine Manhattan*). Inseparable.

This to the annoyance of Max Liebman, the impresario of Caesar's career, and a giant in his own right, a central figure in the story of how American comedy turned Jewish. Liebman, Vienna-born, Brooklyn-raised, had done stints in the oil fields of Texas and the silent film companies of Hollywood before making his bones at the Tamiment resort in the Poconos, running the famous revues there, putting on a Broadway-caliber show packed with songs, pantomimes, satires, every Saturday night—and not the same one, either; you think the audiences who were there all summer would have put up with the same show every week? He'd worked with Caesar, that genius of the mountains, on those revues like *Tars and Spars* that were never quite the perfect showcase for his monumental talent.[27] But now the big time beckoned: here was Sid Caesar, raking in huge money at the nightclubs, and there was this new thing, television, poised to become the biggest thing since radio, and its executives were looking for people with live entertainment experience who could handle new, big shows. People like Liebman and Caesar.

And Liebman knew a mooch, a coattail-rider, when he saw one. Particularly since Brooks was constantly there, constantly making a pest of himself, constantly *wanting*, but also with a lack of any kind of control: he had to joke, he never had a sense of occasion, there was no *discipline*. Which, given the monumentality of the task of putting on these shows, was centrally important. But Caesar liked him—no, more than liked him; Brooks had become near-family—and Liebman was too smart and too experienced a producer to have a scorched-earth fight with his star and meal ticket over something he couldn't win.

So they worked out a compromise. When the Liebman-produced, Caesar-starring *The Admiral Broadway Revue* premiered on television in January 1949, packed with Tamiment talent like Imogene Coca and writers Mel Tolkin and Lucille Kallen and performed in best Tamiment style, Brooks wasn't hired. But Brooks got to hang around nonetheless, sitting there—or, sometimes, right outside the rehearsal room, not allowed in—and throwing out ideas, which Caesar would receive in his lordly fashion and accept or reject as was his whim (and finely and brilliantly honed comic sensibility). And why not? Caesar was paying him fifty dollars a week out of his own pocket, after all. In a later interview, after Brooks had become famous in his own right, Liebman insisted the reason for not paying Brooks was he couldn't find money in the budget: "In the beginning . . . we were so strapped that when Sid asked me to put his young pal, Mel Brooks, on the payroll, I couldn't afford to. So, just to keep him around as court jester, Sid paid him $50 a week out of his own pocket." The budget was indeed very low at the start, but this has more than a whiff of retroactive self-justification.[28]

The Admiral Broadway Revue, in an irony prefiguring *The Producers*, was canceled because it was too successful. Its job was to help raise the profile of its corporate sponsor, a maker of television sets, and it did so well that the company needed all of its cash to manufacture the sets—and couldn't afford to sponsor the program. But of course no one was going to let the white-hot Caesar go for long, and he returned to television on *Your Show of Shows* in February of 1950, on Saturday nights at nine—a ninety-minute live show every week in prime time. Fitting in ambit for Caesar, that man of gigantic appetites in every way.

Early television, like early work in many new media, had significant continuities with its predecessors. Shows like *Playhouse 90* worked at first because they took the familiar, in this case the theatrical enterprise, and transposed it as seamlessly as possible to the new technology. Audiences—and critics, by and large—were used to appreciating what they had, and while they adjusted to the small screen's potentialities, they wanted more of the same. This was largely true of early television comedy, too: its most successful practitioners were frequently revisiting the kinds of work they could have done—or in fact *had* done—on Borscht Belt stages or in nightclub acts. Like Milton Berle, who'd bowed in with the Texaco Star Theater in 1948, half a year before *The Admiral Broadway Revue*, the same year the RCA 630, "the first good model of a TV set," 375 dollars for a ten-inch screen, came on the market.[29] Or Groucho Marx, who'd come to prominence in live vaudeville long before he and his brothers became film stars.

And so, not surprisingly, many of these early talents were Jews. Part of it was those networks of local entertainment that provided personnel in the New York area, television's birthplace. Part of it was television's comparatively low social and cultural status—the same lack of barriers to entry that enabled Jews to play central roles in emerging mass cultural media from nickelodeons to comic books. But some of it, maybe, had to do with television's particular gifts of reaching out to people where they were, giving them what they wanted, allowing them to connect with the performers in a way the aloof, iconic stars and sirens of the movies couldn't. Caesar's show wasn't called *My Show of Shows*, after all. It was yours.

This invitation of television stars into viewers' living rooms, this kind of increasing cultural domesticity, found its echoes in Caesar's domestic skits, playing off Imogene Coca and Nanette Fabray in skewed, occasionally barbed slice-of-life sketches like the Hickenloopers. (Caesar's contemporary Molly Goldberg brought her more cozily *heymish* version to the small screen, transplanting her hugely successful show from the radio to create, in *The Goldbergs*, one of the foundational sitcoms.) But there was a second way in which Caesar and his writers took the bigger cultural world and writ it small, one far more important to Brooks's later career: via the parody.

One of the twentieth century's most famous literary critics, the Harvard-trained son of Jewish immigrants M. H. Abrams, suggested all literature was either a mirror or a lamp: either trying to reflect reality or indicate the luminous depths of the creative individual. If you were looking for a similar metaphorical choice when it came to Caesar's comedy—and maybe any comedy—the mirror would do just fine, but you'd have to replace the lamp with a pair of backwards binoculars. Comedy is either about recognizing the familiar—the basis of all observational comedy, like those Hickenloopers—or cutting the epic, the pretentious, the unselfconscious, down to size. Is this a particularly Jewish concern? Not at all: Aristophanes' ancient Greek comedies do the same thing, taking on the scholasticism of a contemporary named Socrates. But there's no question that Jews, thanks to the vicissitudes of diaspora history, have long been peculiarly and particularly positioned to examine the structures, conventions, and foibles of a particular society and culture that they are only partially of, and then try to poke at them. And they do so—it must always be said—out of some kind of love, or at least attraction, or fascination. Only these sentiments yield the kind of attention necessary to successful parody.

But how, precisely? And how Jewishly? What does it *mean* when Caesar, in his parody of the Western *Shane*, explains his powerful thirst on the grounds that he'd eaten a herring for breakfast? Or when he plays the silent film icon who almost couldn't transition to talkies because of his silly high-pitched voice? (Which, thankfully, lowers when he catches a cold, meaning he—and thus Caesar—were doused with water, over and over again, before important "takes.") How about the occasional Yiddishisms smuggled into seemingly innocuous skits, like "Japanese" characters named *Gehakte leber* ("Chopped Liver") and so forth? Are these signs of a secret Jewish language coursing through the veins of *Your Show of Shows*? Comments on anxieties of Jewish masculinity, the way disguised ethnicity lay behind so much of the framework of imagined American cinematic manhood? A wink and a nod of peekaboo Judaism to a far less universally and geographically distributed—and thus far more proportionately and demographically Jewish—early television audience? (Mel Tolkin, one of the program's lead writers, would often encourage the writers' room to redouble its efforts by saying: "It's Tuesday, and hundreds of Jews all over America are waiting to see what we'll do [on Saturday]."[30]

Or was it just the jeu d'esprit of that fearsome writers' room? Some of the most famous of Caesar's alumni—Woody Allen, Larry Gelbart—never actually wrote for *Your Show of Shows*; they worked on its successor, *Caesar's Hour.* But the tone was set by the time they arrived, by writers like Tolkin, co-star Carl Reiner (who often joined for writing sessions), Neil Simon, Lucille Kallen, and, of course, Brooks. Writers unquestionably intellectual in their ambitions and their experiences—seeking out new aesthetic frontiers like the Italian neorealist cinema or Japanese film on view four blocks away at afternoon screenings in the Museum of Modern Art, even if, as would become clear in some ways, their immediate response to internalizing it was to mine it for parodic appeal.[31] Tolkin encouraged the young Brooks, "Big Mel" to "Little Mel," to read Tolstoy and Gogol, leading the fledgling writer with big ambitions to become nothing less than "the American Molière, the new Aristophanes." Later, when that ambition was arguably fulfilled, Brooks had a portrait of Tolstoy in his office; when Tolkin died in 2007, he said, "I was very fortunate to be a student in the Mel Tolkin class."[32]

Brooks was in that writers' room from the beginning. Not as a writer, though; Liebman had seen to that, at least at first. When his first credit appeared, a crawl on the seventh episode of *Your Show of Shows* reading "Additional Dialogue by Mel Brooks," you could practically feel its grudging nature coming off the screen in waves. And that first credited material was nothing special—Caesar playing a Stanislavski disciple named Ivano Ivanovich who demonstrates the Method by pretending to be a pinball in a pinball machine, rendering Romeo and Juliet in typical Caesar Russian gibberish, gags pitched high and low. In the summer of 1950, Brooks was serving as a social director at Grossinger's, writing the staff show.[33]

But he was a dominant presence in the writers' room even from the start: popping Raisinets, sharing details from his four-times-a-week therapy sessions (begun during the summer of 1951 on Tolkin's advice), pitching lines, jokes, ideas at a mile a minute, most of them dross, some pure gold. And Brooks, when he was convinced something was good, would pursue it relentlessly: given his relationship to Caesar, he felt comfortable popping into the great man's dressing room before the show and whispering some of his favorite rejected lines, hoping Caesar would toss them in during the live broadcast. Brooks even punched Caesar once to get his attention, hardly a risk-free stratagem: the oft-repeated, apparently true account that Caesar dangled Brooks out a window is a case in point.

In the 1976 Mel Brooks film *Silent Movie*, there is a scene between him and Caesar. In the movie, Brooks, playing a film director, comes to pitch his boss, a studio head played by Caesar, on an idea. The idea—in a typical Brooks meta-conceit—is a silent movie, like the one we viewers are watching now. Brooks presents the idea, then stands there, hands splayed out, eyes wide open, waiting for reaction: one can imagine him having done the same thing, a quarter-century before, over and over again, with this joke and a thousand others, a hammy, Jewish show-bizzy, "Hah?? Hahh??" Caesar, wan and shriveled on a hospital bed—a shadow of his former self that wasn't nearly all acting; alcoholism, particularly, had taken its toll—does not react well.

One of the Brooks jokes that became a byword for comedy death on *Your Show of Shows* provides the glimmerings of a divergence in sensibility between the two and a future artistic path forward for the younger comedian. In Brooks's joke, a man walks through a zoo and stops while in the reptile house, taken aback by the sound of a snake calling to him. In Brooks's language, ventriloquizing Caesar: "You see that snake in there? Ja? Vell, he don't vant to be in dere. I passed by the snake cage and that snake whispered to me 'You gotta get me out of here. This place is full of snakes!' And I looked at him and said, 'Vhat you want out for? You're a snake, too!'"[34]

Caesar, genius that he was, was right and wrong about the joke. He was wrong if he didn't appreciate the joke, because it's brilliant: in many ways, it's the encapsulation of the Jewish condition in postwar America, trying hard to make it by being like everyone else and then realizing that that means . . . being like everybody else, which it's simply impossible to be. As comedian, as artist, as Jew, take your pick. But Caesar was also right: because this level of complex identification and dis-identification, of expressing dissonance with his audience, was never his shtick. Even his coterie of oddball authorities and showy strongmen leads were just costumes: that was our Sid up there performing, one of us that made good—whoever "us" happened to be. But Brooks was, would be, something very much else again.

By the second season of *Your Show of Shows*, Brooks was a full-fledged writer, focusing particularly—and unsurprisingly—on the movie and film parodies that were becoming a regular, practically structured part of the show.[35] And by midway through that season, the show, its star, and its owner-producer Liebman were on top of the world. In March 1952, NBC was offering half-hour fall season sponsorships of the ninety-minute program for $55,000 per half hour. A one-minute commercial at the half-hour mark was available for $17,600 a minute; or for the 52-week season for one million dollars, close to ten times that in today's money.[36] And Brooks was as close with Caesar as ever. In February, Brooks had been there "pac[ing] the floor" with Caesar, one of his "five inseparable friends"—the others being Reiner, Tolkin, Kallen, and Howard Morris—when Caesar's wife gave birth to a baby boy.[37] The next month, *Variety* spotted him vacationing with Caesar in Miami Beach.[38]

But it was clear that Brooks was already looking to expand his horizons. One reason for the search might be suggested in an article by radio and TV writer and columnist Goodman Ace, in the following month's *Saturday Review*. Ace noted that *Variety*, in reviewing *Your Show of Shows*, mentioned lots of staff members by name, but credited only "the corps of writers." Ace corrected this slight in a column dedicated to championing writers' credits more generally, singling out Tolkin, Brooks, and Kallen by name, but this may have rankled.[39] What seems to have been an attempt to smooth things over may not have quite done the trick: in *Variety*'s forty-seventh anniversary issue, dated January 7, 1953, *Your Show of Shows* took out a celebratory six-page spread.[40] Readers could see full-page pictures of Caesar, Coca, and Liebman, and smaller pictures of Carl Reiner and the Billy Williams Quartet, even the costume designer Paul Du Pont. But in a quarter page on the bottom right-hand corner, there is this: "You mean the show is not AD LIB? No, it's written by— MEL TOLKIN, LUCILLE KALLEN, MEL BROOKS." Big enough letters, but no pictures. One can imagine the young Mel Brooks looking at it, galled and resolute.

Early in 1952, Brooks had provided sketch material for an "intimate revue" starring Eddie Cantor's next but youngest daughter, Marilyn, which was headed to Broadway.[41] The show, with a Philadelphia tryout, was backed by, among others, Cantor, Milton Berle, Jimmy Durante, and Jenny Grossinger, deepening Brooks's connection with other members of the great and the good of American popular entertainment and Jewish showbiz royalty.[42] (Although, in the small world that was Jewish life at the time, there was also a personal connection: Brooks's mother Kitty had briefly dated Cantor as a teenager, and as a child, Brooks had attended a New Jersey camp for underprivileged kids Cantor had funded.)[43] *Variety*'s out-of-town review suggested the show needed a lot of work, including "more comedy material"; it did note, however, "a hilarious burlesque of 'Death of a Salesman'," which had itself premiered just three years before.[44] That hilarious burlesque, with the Russian-lit title "Of Fathers and Sons," was, unsurprisingly, Brooks's, who would then repurpose it for the show *New Faces of 1952*.[45] In Brooks's telling, the Willy Loman figure is a crook who can no longer steal; his only hope is that his son will follow in his footsteps. But Stanley comes home—the horror—with straight A's. His mother begs him: "Steal something, anything. I know you can. I know, deep down inside where it counts, you're rotten." But it's not to be.

Arthur Miller attended the show, and was said to have enjoyed the sketch; it may be too much, or perhaps just enough, to think his enjoyment stemmed from seeing in the sketch the kind of Jewish-y underpinnings Brooks sensed almost viscerally in the play—the ones Miller would, late in life, suggest, or import, into his midcentury American masterpiece. (In an essay written in 1999, he called the Lomans "Jews light-years away from religion or a community that might have fostered Jewish identity.")[46] Certainly Brooks's affectionate portrait of a kind of cozy, even *heymish* criminal would appear again and again in his work—an American Jewish analogue to the easy riding, raging and bullish anti-heroes who would flourish on American movie screens alongside his characters. But maybe the most important subtext of the sketch, for Brooks's biography, was the one about sons disappointing fathers, distancing themselves from their example: the way Brooks was realizing would, eventually, have to happen between himself and Caesar.

But qualifiedly, at best: during hiatus in 1952, he traveled briefly to Europe with the *Your Show of Shows* crowd. "TV-legit scripter Mel Brooks to Europe for the summer," as *Variety* put it, reflecting Brooks's role and reputation at the time.[47] Scripter. Not performer. His only acting on *Your Show of Shows* was to deliver the screech of a trampled-on cat. Off camera. (And even then, he blew his cue in dress rehearsal.)[48] But far outside of camera range, during summers on Fire Island and at Moss Hart and Kitty Carlisle's dinner parties, he was beginning to perform. With help.

The precise story regarding the creation of Brooks's greatest character, certainly the greatest character he played himself not named Mel Brooks, is slightly obscure. Fair enough; he *is* two thousand years old, after all. Or so he says. But a relatively reliable account comes from Brooks's co-conspirator in the effort, Caesar's reliable scene partner, frequent straight man, and inordinate talent in his own right Carl Reiner. Reiner, like Brooks, had made a great deal of comic hay in the parody field, particularly by interviewing various outrageous Caesar characters under what had once been called "Non-Entities in the News," the most famous of which was the Teutonic know-it-all (humbug) Professor—Brooks's other authorial specialty. As Reiner tells it, one day, in the *Your Show of Shows* writers' room, he turned to Brooks and said, in the tone of the newscaster Dan Seymour from the Sunday night show *We the People*, "Here with us today, ladies and gentlemen, is a man who was actually at the scene of the Crucifixion, two thousand years ago. Isn't that true, sir?" Brooks looked at him, paused, and said, "Oh, boy." And thus began the 2,000-year-old man.[49]

Brooks was so fertile, so alive, in the part, a descendant of and yet entirely other than Caesar's Professor, that he was putting off sparks. "I really wailed. I could hear my antecedents. I could hear five thousand years of Jews pouring through me," he said. "Within a couple of decades, there won't be any more accents like that. They're being ironed out by history. It's the sound I was brought up on, and it's dying."[50] "It's easier to hide behind accents," he said on another occasion. "I can say anything I want, and then if people question me, I say, 'Don't blame me. Blame the old Jew. He's crazy!'"[51] But that crazy Jewish id needed a controlling superego, and Reiner was a master sculptor: shaping him, bringing him back if he went too far afield, nudging him with ideas when he threatened to get stuck, pruning unpromising directions and suggesting new ones. It was a huge hit in the insidery, showbizzy, very Jewish circles of Reiner and Brooks's friends and acquaintances, but both of them felt it would never fly in public. It was, after all, too Jewish.

Not that there hadn't been plenty of vaudeville and burlesque comedy rendered in a Yiddish accent: Smith and Dale, Weber and Fields, Gertrude Berg and Mrs. Bloom. But, as Reiner put it, with Hitler's rise, "Jewish and non-Jewish writers, producers, and performers started to question the Yiddish accent's acceptability as a tool of comedy. The accent had a self-deprecating and demeaning quality that gave aid and comfort to the Nazis. . . . From 1941 on, the Yiddish accent was slowly, and for the most part, voluntarily, phased out of show business."[52] And so it was kept a secret. For the time being. But the inordinately positive response it got could only have encouraged Brooks's own ambitions.

And in addition, the strain was beginning to show on Caesar's program. By that fall of 1952, the ratings had dropped, and advertisers were beginning to leave; by mid-season, they were leaving in greater numbers.[53] By the season's end, in May 1953, *Variety* was reporting that *Your Show of Shows* would return the next season for three out of four weeks, not every week, and with fewer supporting acts: which "should come with a measure of relief to producer Max Liebman," they said. "Even that master revue conferencier, schooled in the grind of Camp Tamiment, Pa., and abetted by such gifted writers as Lucille Kallen, Mel Tolkin, and Mel Brooks, has been finding it tough to sustain the high quality of diamond polish he has sought for 90 minutes, week after week." Which was a polite way of saying that the show was not the must-see event it once had been, despite some all-time great sketches, like the "Birth of a Star" parody Brooks surely had a hand in—"an outstanding number . . . one of the series kidding films, in this case the genre of corny pix on the trials and tribulations of Hollywood stars," *Variety* had raved back in January.[54] Readers were told, in fact, to expect a lot of reprises.

Were there other options for Brooks, escape routes? Hollywood beckoned, and that summer he went west to explore a Caesar-Coca film possibility; like many a Hollywood prospect, it sounded tempting and never materialized. But Brooks landed, or so it seemed, on his feet. *Variety* announced on July 13, 1953, that Columbia Pictures had hired him to write an adaptation of Somerset Maugham's play *Home and Beauty*, a romantic comedy better known under the title of its earlier movie version, *Too Many Husbands*, as a vehicle for Rita Hayworth. Hollywood being what it is, the picture appeared in 1955 with the title *Three for the Show*, starring Betty Grable (and Jack Lemmon). Brooks's name appears nowhere in the credits, unsurprisingly: he lasted one day on the project before being reassigned.[55] But perhaps his hand could be seen—or the reason for hiring him ascertained—in one fundamental and dramatic change from the play, and even from its earlier cinematic adaptation. *Three for the Show* was a musical.

Brooks's take on Hollywood filmed entertainment was presumably well represented in *Your Show of Shows'* fourth full season: *Variety*, in a measured review of the new season's premiere, singled out the program's "hilarious takeoff on 'From Here to Eternity' (their title: 'From Here to Obscurity') that was one of the best of the Caesar-Coca film satires to date."[56] (It also, perhaps coincidentally, featured Caesar getting doused again and again: no one ever took a pail of water to the face like the spluttering Caesar.) Brooks and others, now old hands, were joined by a new burst of writing talent, including Neil Simon and future *Fiddler on the Roof* playwright Joseph Stein. But all good things had to come to an end, and the 1953–1954 season was the last for *Your Show of Shows*. "It is very easy to sentimentalize on the passing from the television scene of NBC's 'Your Show of Shows,'" sentimentalized *Variety* on June 9, 1954: "There had never been a program before or since the natal day of Feb. 25, 1950, that embodied so many show business elements with such skill, imagination, and the truly bigleague touch." But lest there be too much mourning, the show business journal continued, "As Sir Winston Churchill might observe, it's the end of the beginning. The die has been cast, but the cast is not dead." Caesar and Coca would each have their own show. One of which, at least, would certainly have room for Brooks.

While his fate in TV was being settled, though, Brooks continued to seize other opportunities, significantly more prestigious ones at the time. In July 1954 the *New York Times* announced that he was working, along with several other writers, on "Delilah," a Carol Channing theatrical vehicle with a "song and dance plot" and with "a movie background during the 'vamp' span of 1909–1918."[57] "Delilah" combined many of the things that were catnip to Brooks: comedy, music, old movie history. And, perhaps not accidentally, traces of a Black presence: "Delilah" had started life as a prospective musical called "Samson and Lila Dee," "an all-black retelling of the biblical Samson and Delilah story," and changed, as these things do, when no star was found.[58] After various peregrinations, "Delilah" would appear on Broadway in November of the next year under the title *The Vamp*, described by the *Times* as a "Musical Spoofing Silent Film Era." (Channing played "a farm girl who never heard of the movies until a 1913 film company invades her uncle's farm in the Bronx to shoot a Western.")[59] Again, Brooks was uncredited as part of the writing team; but simply because he didn't get the credit doesn't mean it wasn't formative in future efforts.

With his dreams of the Great White Way deferred, Brooks returned to the then lower-status medium of the small screen, giving up—or getting away from—the *Your Show of Shows* circle, and receiving an upgrade in his job title to writer-director in return. But it was a battlefield promotion, for a show clearly in the throes of chaos: when Brooks received his first name in *Daily Variety* headlines on September 30, 1954, it certainly wasn't what he'd have wanted that occasion to look like. "Mel Brooks Resigns from Buttons Vidshow," the headline read.

The career of Red Buttons, if slightly less celebrated than Caesar's, ran along parallel lines. Born Aaron Chwatt to Jewish immigrants in New York, he played the Borscht Belt, worked in entertainment during the war, appearing in an Army Air Forces Show that became a movie, and went into television with his own variety show starting in 1952. It was entering its third and final season when Brooks came on the scene, and it was a production in turmoil: the show had switched networks after being canceled by CBS, and Brooks had been signed as writer-director the week before the show started on NBC, with the former director, Julie Oshins, having been "upped" to executive producer. (This had been part of a regular trend for Buttons: as his ratings had dropped precipitously, he'd been hiring and firing writers left and right.) Clearly, the quick fix didn't work; a note a week later suggested Buttons and Brooks "couldn't see 'script to script' on his Friday nighter," and the return of Oshins to the director's chair suggested fairly standard showbiz infighting, if no less brutal for that.[60]

It's hard to imagine Buttons and Brooks seeing eye to eye: despite the superficial similarities—interests in audience-pleasing, particularly with a song and dance soft shuffle—Brooks had an aggressive comic core that didn't quite mesh with Buttons's impish playfulness. If Buttons can be said, and I'll admit this is

stretching it a bit, to represent a certain kind of totally assimila-
tive style in the American Jewish approach to 1950s comedy—
he played characters named Rocky and Buggsy, for instance,
largely non-ironically—Brooks could never, would never, be
able to take out the snagging thorn, the parodic reminder, the
hint of Jewish alienation. It wasn't a match.

Brooks returned home, or close to it; to Coca's show, rather
than to Caesar's. But the show encountered difficulties right off
the bat, and sputtered out almost immediately. Brooks would
eventually rise to head writer, after Kallen and everyone else
left; but finally he would get the ax, too.[61] His theatrical horizons had also shrunk somewhat; instead of being Broadway
bound with a full-fledged musical, he was working, during the
winter of 1955, on a revue at the small off-Broadway house the
Barbizon Plaza, a venue notable, at least to certain audiences,
for hosting the surprisingly successful *World of Sholom Aleichem*
for an extremely long run just a few months earlier. Brooks
contributed sketches to *Watch the Birdie*, later retitled *Once Over
Lightly*. But there were networking compensations. The revue
was directed by a hot Broadway director—Stanley Prager, who
did *The Pajama Game*—and its star, a gentleman of some off-
Broadway success who went on to attract notice for the televised version of the *Sholom Aleichem* production, was named
Zero Mostel.[62] Their paths would cross again later, but this
seems to be the first time Brooks wrote for Zero.

As exciting and vibrant as writing for the theater might
have been, though, television was more lucrative, and Brooks
had responsibilities: he was almost thirty and about to start a
family—he became a father for the first time in 1956. (He'd
married Florence Baum, a dancer, in 1953.) And Caesar beckoned; unlike Coca's show, his second act, *Caesar's Hour*, looked
"to have staying power." At least that's what *Variety* said, in its
review of the second-season premiere in September 1955, which
featured Brooks's touch. The article singled out for particular

praise a playlet where Coca replacement Nanette Fabray was a torch singer in a Prohibition cabaret setting and "pretended to take off on 'movie' themes in that category"—a classic kind of Brooksian sketch, shades of Madeline Kahn's later bravura performance in *Blazing Saddles*.[63] And the critics continued to approve; Brooks received his first Emmy nomination that year, along with fellow writers Mel Tolkin, Selma Diamond, Larry Gelbart, and Sheldon Keller.

To give a sense of the Jewishness of early television: of the five shows in Brooks's category of Best Comedy Writing, three of them featured classic, albeit not necessarily explicit, exemplars of midcentury American Jewish comedy: Caesar, Jack Benny, and Phil Silvers. (The other two, no slouches themselves, were the writers for *I Love Lucy* and the now comparatively forgotten *George Gobel Show*.) Television was still a smaller medium, both geographically and demographically speaking, and still sufficiently a New York enterprise that, although the ceremonies were televised, they were joint affairs at the Waldorf-Astoria in New York and the Pan-Pacific auditorium in Los Angeles, the latter made to look like the Waldorf via "elaborate sets." "Diners" would be "watching activity at both ends of the continent via television."[64]

Those diners, along with Brooks and his fellow writers, got to watch Phil Silvers's team win, for their skills at summoning into life the *hondling*, scheming Sgt. Bilko, as much a product of the frantic businessmen of Sholem Aleichem's fiction so beloved by producer Nat Hiken as of the vaudeville acts Silvers had come up in. And they watched them win again the following year, in a near repeat of the contest, speaking both generally and Jewishly (eliminate George Gobel and Lucy from the nominees; insert Ernie Kovacs and Perry Como). And then they watched them win *again* in 1958, in another near repeat of the contest (this time remove just Perry Como and insert *Father Knows Best*). No wonder Brooks—never a man to take his fate quietly—took to the top of his table and the top of his lungs at the 1957 ceremony when the names of the winning writers were announced, shouting: "Coleman Jacoby and Arnie Rosen won an Emmy and Mel Brooks didn't. Nietzsche was right. There is no God! There is no God!"[65]

Maybe, just maybe, he was also still feeling a little resentful of his own proximate, personified Deity. On March 20, 1957, near the end of what proved to be his show's final season, Caesar had taken out a full-page ad in *Variety*. "My sincere thanks to my great writing staff who helped so much to make the awards possible," "Sid" wrote. He then listed them in this order: Tolkin, Gelbart, Brooks, Simon, Keller, Stewart, Belkin. *Third-billed? Big Mel, all right, but Gelbart, that newcomer, ahead of me?* But the writing was on the wall, anyway; nominations notwithstanding, the show was canceled by that May. There would be specials and one-offs in the future, but for all intents and purposes Caesar's reign was at an end.

He left the television landscape almost inconceivably different from where he'd found it. In 1948, just before *The Admiral Broadway Revue* premiered, there'd been 175,000 television sets in operation in the country. When *Caesar's Hour* was up, there were 44 million, roughly one for every four Americans, and "the average televiewer" was watching it "6.07 hours a day."[66] Movies, radio, comic books—increasingly, the other foundations of mass culture would have to contract to accommodate the new small screen giant.

As would Brooks's great love, the theater, whose role as mass entertainment venue had been shrinking since vaudeville, even as the 1950s marked a golden age in combining crowd-pleasing entertainment with aesthetic accomplishment in the medium. In 1957, here was what was on offer for the Broadway-goer: *Auntie Mame; Bells Are Ringing; Brigadoon; Damn Yankees; The Diary of Anne Frank; The Happiest Millionaire; Inherit the Wind; Long Day's Journey into Night*, starring Fredric March;

Major Barbara with Charles Laughton and Burgess Meredith; *The Most Happy Fella; My Fair Lady;* and *No Time For Sergeants.* Into that murderers' row of material stepped Mel Brooks, with a musical adaptation of a newspaper column about a talking cockroach and a cat.

Don Marquis had created archy and mehitabel for the New York *Evening Sun* in the 1910s. The gist of the entirely uncategorizable column was that archy, a sentient and soulful cockroach, had gotten into the habit of writing column copy on a typewriter in the *Evening Sun* office once everyone had left for the night by jumping up and down on the keys. (He couldn't jump on the shift key at the same time as a different letter: as a result, everything, including his name, was in lowercase.) His practice was to comment on city life along with a faithful feline friend of his named mehitabel. The popular columns became even more so when they were collected in book form during the late 1920s and '30s—that is, they were at their height of fame during Brooks's childhood, the epitome of a certain kind of New York knowingness. (It's arch: he's *called* archy, after all.)

George Kleinsinger, probably best known as the composer of the kids' piece "Tubby the Tuba," loved Marquis's works; along with writer Joe Darion, he'd produced a musical version of the work on record around the time Brooks was working on "Delilah" for Channing in the mid-1950s. Thus, almost certainly, the overlap: the Kleinsinger/Darion record starred Channing as a brassy mehitabel, along with Preston Sturges alum Eddie Bracken as archy. There had been various live performances of the record, and now, finally, in 1957, it looked like there was going to be a successful effort to bring the show to Broadway, under the title *Shinbone Alley,* the name of an actual small streetlet in New York. (It's near Bleecker and Lafayette, and was formerly known as Jones Alley.)[67]

Brooks, continuing his run of penning musical adaptations of unlikely source material, was brought on to help Darion punch up the book, the team adding "five new tunes and lyrics," according to the *Times*.[68] As of six days before the planned April 13 premiere, he would be co-credited with the book. The production was opening in the nineteen-hundred-seat Broadway Theater without a road tryout, financed at a little under a quarter of a million dollars; with a top ticket price of $7.50, *Variety* noted, it could "break even at about 34,000 gross."[69] It didn't. It closed on May 25 after forty-nine performances.

The trouble started, or, at least, boiled over, four days before the Saturday night opening, when *Shinbone Alley*'s director Norman Lloyd quit. "The withdrawal was attributed by Mr. Lloyd to 'a great difference of opinion regarding the approach to the show' with Peter Lawrence, sponsor [producer], and the writers, Joe Darion and Mel Brooks," the *Times* reported, along with the news that Lawrence felt it "will not be necessary to engage another director."[70] That probably meant Lawrence himself took over as director, though neither he nor anyone else was credited; Lloyd had asked for his name to be taken off the production.[71]

While the paper of record didn't give any details about what the difference of opinion between the parties actually was, the clue lay in the message on the frontispiece to the manuscript of the play: "Although our characters are insects and animals, the problems they face and the emotions they feel are those of human beings. The players on our stage will therefore be dressed as human beings. Animal or insect characteristics will be revealed, musically, in lyrics and dance."[72] Characterization would be remarkably difficult with this kind of set-up at the best of times; what the creative team had been given to work with was, at best, a situation—the kind you could imagine Caesar doing in one of his *Your Show of Shows* sketches, where he mugged and pretended to *be* an animal. Yes, raw physicality and grace were there, most notably in the presence of Eartha Kitt, who played mehitabel, and the talent bench ran deep: Bracken reprised his role as archy, and both a pre–*West Side Story* Chita Rivera and a pre–Bob Newhart Tom Poston were standbys in the production. And indeed, there were plenty of funny bits and spectacle, including a fifteen-foot typewriter for archy to jump on.[73] But all of that was hard to translate into more than a few minutes of comic enjoyment. What you needed was a coherent plot, rather than a collection of jokes and moments: and Darion and Brooks didn't seem to have come up with one.

Brooks Atkinson, in his review, credited Kleinsinger, Darion, and Brooks for trying "to use the theatre to create a world of sardonic fantasy," but noted that while they'd "arranged some odd and interesting episodes, they have not been able to pull the work together, especially in that second act, which slowly disintegrates."[74] In a later rumination, he was actively negative about Brooks and Darion's work: "Not much of the humorous comment on human nature is left in the libretto of 'Shinbone Alley.' A librettist would have to be the equivalent of Don Marquis to bring it into the theatre. What Mr. Darion and Mr. Brooks have done on their own account is not a satisfactory substitute."[75] *Variety* was even less appreciative. "Offhand," its review opened, "you might think it would be just about impossible to do a good musical show about a cockroach and an alley cat. How right you'd be!" There were murmurs of faint praise—Thomas R. Dash of *Women's Wear Daily* remarked that "Joe Darion and Mel Brooks, the architects of the book, have whipped together a simple but disarming libretto," and *Newsday* critic George Oppenheimer singled out "some sparkling lines" by Brooks and his writing partner (while believing the first-rate moments were "lost in a maze of mediocrity").[76] But John Chapman, who had enjoyed the show more than most of the critics, summed it up best in his annual *Broadway's Best* volume: "The reviews were mixed, for some of the critics were unwilling to go along with the whimsy."[77]

As such, the reviews intrigue now for their foreshadowing

of so much of the negative critique of Brooks's later filmmaking. Sacrificing character and plot for jokes and spectacle, individual brilliant moments in a work that fails to sustain an even tone: all this would come to form a regular chorus for those who failed, in Chapman's words, "to go along with the whimsy." Or, in other ways, to spot the serious intent and ambition beneath. It is worth noting, though, that *Shinbone Alley* featured one important and "impressive" milestone, one which also would resonate a few years later, when Brooks hit it big. "If offhand memory is correct," *Variety*'s critic mused, "it's the first Broadway musical to use a Negro-white cast indiscriminately. Since it involves only insects and animals, who haven't been 'educated' about skin pigmentation, the show's racial mixture is quite logical. The fact that it seems just a matter of course would, natch, give a Dixiecrat apoplexy."[78] (The first *off*-Broadway show to use race-blind casting had been *The World of Sholom Aleichem*.) The seeds of later trends were beginning to emerge: the complexities of race, certainly, but even more so the frustrations and the chaos of the theater.

At almost the precise moment the play opened—April 9, 1957—Brooks, along with a number of other comedy writers, was contacted by Marie Torre, a *Herald Tribune* reporter, for reactions to the indications that "the pendulum of TV preoccupation will shift next season from comedians to singers." Brooks, looking to build a career and support a family, is reported as pointing out that "comedy writers easily adjust to the vicissitudes of the industry"—if they don't write for comedians, they can write for variety hosts.[79] Whether Brooks knew it for certain or was merely prophesying, his next television job after *Caesar's Hour* ended was, indeed, for a variety host.

Polly Bergen was riding high in the late 1950s, after a string of movie roles starting as an unnamed singer and working her way up, as a regular recording artist with Columbia Records, a lauded spot as a regular on *To Tell the Truth*, and then a 1957

Emmy-winning performance—at a time when Brooks was still in the throes of his losses to Silvers's writers—for a *Playhouse 90* version of *The Helen Morgan Story*, playing the Broadway actress and torch singer who suffered from, and eventually succumbed to, alcoholism. Given the chance to headline her own television show, when the premiere episode tanked, "Bergen heaved out the writers and producers of her opening dud," the *Daily Defender* noted, "and hired Sid Caesar's sense of humor, Mel Brooks, to write and produce this week's comeback."[80]

In light of the arc of Brooks's own career, his personal life, his own relationships with strong leading ladies in every sense of the word, and his many, many investigations into the ins and outs of Jewish masculinity (and Jewish gender more generally), it's worth remembering both that Brooks cut his creative teeth on shows with strong female leads and that the early television landscape—perhaps to a degree even surprising today—was full of variety shows headed by women. And not just Coca and Lucille Ball, either; Polly Bergen's year was, as a critic for *Cosmopolitan* noted, the year of the "girl-singer mistress of ceremonies," with Dinah Shore, Gisele MacKenzie, Bergen, Patti Page, and Rosemary Clooney all having their own shows.[81]

And this one, at first, seemed like it might be Brooks's ticket. *Variety* would report a week later that, "After a somewhat shaky start two weeks earlier, the alternate-Saturday 'Polly Bergen Show' straightened out last weekend into a slick music & comedy offering. . . . Show has been having its production problems, but with Mel Brooks now ensconced as producer and writer, and Bill Colleran holding down the director end, much of the problems now seem out of the way." The show's comedy guest, Ernie Kovacs, undoubtedly helped make it "a snappy and clean half-hour, a rare commodity these days."[82] Kovacs, one of early television's seminal (non-Jewish) comedians, became a favorite for his surreal sight gags that used the new medium to its most expansive capacities. Sometimes they relied on camera tricks, and sometimes—as in the case of the Nairobi Trio, a threesome of apes sporting derbies—they were simply odd. (On the Bergen episode, the Trio appeared to play Beethoven's Fifth with a full-scale symphony orchestra.)

This was a very different kind of comedy from Caesar's, both technically proficient and proudly outsider, and Brooks certainly took note—especially when Kovacs, in his own show that year, was nominated for multiple Emmy awards, and Brooks wasn't. Brooks—who later called Kovacs "a comedy genius" and the most neglected TV artist in history—would never become a full-fledged surrealist, but the cramming of sight gags into his movies is a complicated combination of the showbiz anything-for-a-laugh philosophy, the studied careful technique of this early TV pioneer, and the shotgun "chicken-fat" technique of Will Elder and the other (almost always Jewish) gang of idiots at *Mad Magazine*, just then beginning its long reign of corrupting the minds of American youth.[83] After all, things that look like throwaway jokes in movies are almost always very carefully constructed product.

Brooks's initial success on the show notwithstanding, he was soon replaced as producer. While this may not have necessarily had to do solely with Brooks—the winter of 1957 saw a TV "mass show-doctoring spree," where lots of sponsors and contracted agencies were moving players around to fix their properties—it still couldn't have felt good.[84] Brooks had the opportunity to briefly return to the womb once more—co-writing a Caesar-Coca show airing on ABC in January 1958, sponsored by that great Jewish business entrepreneur Helena Rubinstein.[85] But *Variety*, intentionally or not, twisted the knife: though the show was "way off," it said, it didn't matter to Caesar and Coca fans, who put their trust in chemistry—and in the power of nostalgia. "It's one of the peculiar phenomena of a medium that, barely a dozen years old, can still speak of 'major comebacks' and welcome back 'vets.' Such is the telescoping of time and fame on video."[86] One network executive, under the cover of anonymity, was blunter about Caesar and the sketch comedian entertainment world he represented, describing the show as "the thrashing about of the dinosaur in the marshes of evolution."[87]

Brooks must have been wondering whether he would ever be able to succeed without hitching himself to Caesar, and now whether he was already washed up at thirty-one, fundamentally attached to part of a nostalgic enterprise. His personal life was also flailing. At the end of 1958, Brooks's second child and first son was born. He and Florence named him Nicholas, after Nikolai Gogol, a joint decision that belied the increasing stresses on the marriage, in no small part thanks to Brooks's infidelities. (One of the most notable affairs was with Eartha Kitt, during the production of *Shinbone Alley*.)[88] Soon after this, Brooks would separate from Florence and move in with his more straitlaced friend Speed Vogel; some later said the resulting conflicts inspired Neil Simon's play *The Odd Couple*. Florence filed for divorce in 1960, claiming, in her request for alimony, physical and verbal abuse, degradation, and adulterous relationships.[89]

Brooks pleaded near-poverty in setting the terms of the divorce, which was finalized at the start of 1962, and whatever the precise fiscal circumstances were, his professional career certainly wasn't that of a show-business success. Brooks's produced credits in 1959 and 1960 were largely a series of undistinguished television specials. With Big Mel, he wrote for an NBC telecast in February 1959, *The Lighter Side of Love*, which starred among others the new smash improv duo Mike Nichols and Elaine May.[90] The two also wrote for Ginger Rogers and a spring show starring the British comedian David King. King's show, *Newsday* reported, featured a sketch comparing New York and London policemen and "the plight of a stranger caught in a Manhattan subway." "Neither of the sketches was particularly original. The subway interlude in fact smacked of similar spoofs we've seen on television"—not least, it could be noted, on Caesar's own programs.[91] It felt imitative, exhausted. No less repetitive were the specials he actually worked on for Caesar, one of which, it should be noted for the history books, marked "the first official collaboration between Brooks and Woody Allen," twenty-three years old at the time; the novice writer would often accompany the old hand on long post-writing-session walks from Rockefeller Center to Brooks's place on Fifth and Eighty-seventh.[92]

But there were inklings of things that would come to fruition in the decade to come. In the spring of 1959, before the divorce, Brooks showed Florence a work in progress: pages of "An Olde English Novel" about two English producers who produce intentionally awful stage plays.[93] And then in the fall, in late October 1959, the playwright Moss Hart—the son of Jewish immigrants who had invented himself, along with his frequent collaborator George S. Kaufman, as the apotheosis of genteel, boulevardier American wit in plays like *You Can't Take It With You* and *The Man Who Came to Dinner*—threw a party.

It was to celebrate the publication of his autobiography, *Act One*, at Mamma Leone's in New York, and the guest list of two hundred included Marlene Dietrich, Claudette Colbert, Alec Guinness, Rosalind Russell, and Betty Comden and Adolph Green, among many other bold-faced names. Phil Silvers was the master of ceremonies. And Hart asked Brooks to perform, before this august audience, the 2,000-Year-Old Man character he'd done at earlier parties, this time as Hart's ostensibly two-thousand-year-old psychoanalyst. To add to the pressure, Brooks's regular scene partner, Carl Reiner, was across the country, in Hollywood; Big Mel agreed to fill in. "Their faces," observer Kenneth Tynan noted, "were among the few in the room that were not instantly recognizable." It says something about the nature of Brooks's perspective, his concerns and anxieties as an entertainer, that his flop sweat manifested in an insistence on ethnic disguise. Immediately before going on, he

informed Tolkin that "he was not going to play the shrink Jewish."
But then he did, and got his first laugh, and he never went back.
Asked what Hart talked about in his therapy sessions,
Brooks replied: "He talks smut. He talks dirty, he talks filthy,
he talks pure, unadulterated smut. It makes me want to puke."
After hearing the definition of the Oedipus complex—"the dirt-
iest thing I ever heard":

> BROOKS: Where do you get that filth?
> TOLKIN: It comes from a famous play by Sophocles.
> BROOKS: Was he Jewish?
> TOLKIN: No, sir, he was Greek.
> BROOKS: With a Greek, who knows? But with a Jew, you don't do
> a thing like that even to your wife, let alone your mother.[94]

Working Jewish, working blue, working aggressive—all three
mixed together at that restaurant, standing before, and up to,
the cultural great and good. (It was the 2,000-Year-Old Man,
after all, who would later serve as the mouthpiece for the seminal Brooksian insight that tragedy is when I cut my finger, and
comedy is when you fall into an open sewer and die.)[95] Maybe
Brooks had that triumphant performance in mind a few months
later, at the start of 1960, with his first extended appearance on
television.[96]

David Susskind was one of the early visionary producers of
quality television; his programs were dedicated to substantive,
searching examinations of topics of the day. A flagship program, *Open End*, was so called because there was no ending time;
the network simply allowed the nighttime program to run until
it was finished.[97] This was, of course, a boon to those blessed
with the gift of gab, *yiddishe* and otherwise, and one of the most
storied examples of the storied program came on February 21,
1960, when Susskind hosted "Always Leave Them Laughing,"
a discussion with a group of comedy writers including both
Mels, Gelbart, Sheldon Keller, and Charles Andrews, all writ-

ers for Caesar, and Jack Douglas, who wrote for Bob Hope and Red Skelton. Brooks, unsurprisingly, was loquacious, passionate, and opinionated. And his passions and opinions ran highest and strongest on the question of dangerous comedy. Bob Hope, he said, was "never really dangerous. . . . Hope is America's pet, America's puppy." "Nobody can get hurt watching the show," he said about Loretta Young.[98] By contrast, naturally, he presented himself as a "dangerous" comedy writer.

At that time, this was a hard case for Brooks to make for himself on any objective grounds. This was the era of "sick" comedians like Lenny Bruce, who were making jokes about Lawrence Welk interviewing junkies and tossing out Yiddish-sprinkled obscenities, or obscenity-inflected Yiddishisms. *Mad Magazine* was corroding the minds of America's youth by holding nothing sacred, particularly white-picket-fence domesticity as portrayed, and commodified, by Madison Avenue. Nichols and May and Jules Feiffer were ripping the smug self-satisfaction of the bohemian bourgeois to shreds on the stages of Manhattan and in the pages of the *Village Voice*. If Brooks wanted to present himself in the company of these far more genuinely dangerous Jewish comics, he'd have to do a lot more than take on *goyim* like Bob Hope and Loretta Young on a civically minded television program.

And he did, in the decade to come. Oh, boy, did he.

2

What Next, Cancer?

THE 1960s started out slow and unpromising for Brooks, with reminders of failure everywhere he looked. There was the collapse in his personal life; and *Shinbone Alley's* appearance on TV as the play of the week, with *Newsday's* critic chiming in to remind him of the consensus that the book was "painfully slow," and the *Times*, while allowing it was "occasionally appealing," noting that "occasionally" is "the operative word," was a small-screen sign his career was stalling.[1] And a new, potentially hugely promising opportunity to team up with one of the titans of American, and Jewish, comedy would barely last the summer.

In late June of 1960, the *Times* reported that Brooks had been hired to write the screenplay for Jerry Lewis's next movie, *The Ladies' Man*, where Lewis "will portray the only male employee in a girls' boarding house in Hollywood."[2] This would be the follow-up to *The Bellboy*, where Lewis, who'd reached his global fame as part of a double act with Dean Martin, had finally come fully into his own—it was the first movie Lewis had directed himself. During its production, Lewis developed the now-standard "video assist" system, where the filmmaker could watch a take immediately after filming to see if any adjustments were necessary. This was particularly important if the director was also a performer—as in Lewis's case, and, eventually, in Brooks's.

Brooks had worked for Lewis before, helping write a television special for him in 1958; and was acquainted first-hand with the difficulties of working with the famously challenging writer-director-star. But a gig was a gig—at the lordly pay of three thousand dollars a week for four months, no less. Plus, it offered another close-up look at writing Jewish physical comedy from a very different perspective than writing for Caesar: if Caesar was the comedy of surprisingly potent masculinity, with just a hint of impersonator anxiety beneath, Lewis was shlubby neurosis writ large, all mugging and gap teeth and jerky elbows and flailing limbs. While both comedians gave exquisitely controlled physical performances, Caesar partook more of the classical symphony; Lewis was big band. Literally: Lewis's preferred writing partner for his sight gags was the screenwriting neophyte Bill Richmond, an old friend and big-band drummer. By August, Brooks was sharing writing credit with Richmond; by summer's end, after running afoul of Lewis's unwillingness to take his suggestions and his ire for Brooks's chronic punctuality issues and time spent talking on the telephone with Carl Reiner, Brooks was off the project entirely. His draft was entirely rewritten, and he received no credit on the final film.[3]

But while he was on the West Coast, reunited with Reiner, he went to another party. (Reiner was working on a show he would star in called *Head of the Family*, based on his experiences working for Caesar; the show, de-Judaized, recast, and renamed after its new star, eventually went on to television immortality as *The Dick Van Dyke Show*.) The party, thrown by the playwright and screenwriter Joe Fields—himself the son of the famous Jewish vaudevillian Lew Fields, born Lewis Maurice Shanfield—had as its purpose introducing the 2,000-Year-Old Man sketch to the Left Coast. And that was where George Burns and Steve Allen saw it.

Even then, Burns had been in show business forever; he and Gracie Allen had just finished their eight-year run on television in 1958, which had followed their run on radio since 1932, when Brooks was six. They had their format—Allen the illogical font of constant laughs; Burns the brilliantly bemused straight man—and they played it like Stradivarii. But Gracie had retired from show business, and Burns was still hungry, and he told Brooks and Reiner that if they didn't commit the bit to record, he would steal it and do it himself. There were other accounts of the straw that changed the camel's mind, of convincing Brooks and Reiner that it wasn't too provincial. A favorite is the one where Cary Grant asked for a copy of one of the early recordings; and then that raffish Englishman played it, so he said, for the Queen, who professed, at least in Grant's account, to enjoy it immensely. And if it was good enough for the Queen, well. More prosaically, Steve Allen underwrote a recording session for a commercial release. "If you don't like it, burn it or throw it away," Allen said. "But at least get it down."[4]

There were other, less star-studded reasons for Brooks's change of heart, ones that necessitate some broader historical context. The idea of Cary Grant's playing the recordings for friends (some of royal acquaintance) tells a part of the tale: the recent development of long-playing records that allowed a nightclub-length act to be recorded and presented in its entirety at home. This was particularly important given that Greatest Generation listeners were now home at night raising their Boomer kids—and that another early venue for exposure was less important than it used to be. In an interview when the recording came out, Reiner said: "It's the only medium for young comedians to get the kind of exposure they used to get on radio," and the 1960 article he's quoted in backs him up: "Music stores are plentifully stocked with recordings of young comedians doing their nightclub acts and other material that would have been a riot on radio 15 years ago. . . . Each record amounts to a half-hour comedy show."[5]

This was crucial for Reiner and Brooks: the nature of the 2,000-Year-Old Man act—the build, the improvisation, the sheer exhaustive magnitude of the genius highwire act—is best appreciated at greater length, rather than as a single joke. It's also best appreciated, certainly before Brooks became more polished as a physical performer, as a disembodied voice (or, as was briefly the case in the 1970s, as an animated cartoon figure). Watching Brooks perform the character in a funny cape and hat, as he did in his early television appearances, takes the viewer out of the illusion. Brooks—at least at the time—is *channeling* an old Jew, but doesn't *embody* one, and so doesn't do justice to his ideas and his voice. He himself would say, in an interview almost fifteen years later: "I watched every [*Your Show of Shows*] live for many years, and I wanted to do it but I didn't have the guts so I used to do it at parties to show them how good I was. . . . But I never had the guts to risk it in front of those high school kids that said 'You're full of shit.' I was afraid of the public. I knew the business would love me, but the public, that was a whole other thing. So the safest thing to do was a record because let them break the record, they couldn't break your nose, y'know."[6]

That long-playing technology was also now being used to feature comedy records that weren't necessarily to everyone's taste. That same article had suggested that consumers could pick up records by "sick" comics like Mort Sahl, Shelley Berman, and Jonathan Winters (misspelling the last two names); it almost certainly wouldn't have suggested picking up under-the-counter dirty records by "unkosher comediennes" like Belle

Barth, but plenty of people did—Barth's records sold hundreds of thousands of copies to Jews and Gentiles alike eager to hear sex jokes and smutty double entendres in the privacy of their own homes.

One could argue, perhaps, that Barth's Jewishness was incidental to her appeal—although given the suffusion of Yiddish and American Jewish content it's a very hard argument to make—but it would be impossible to suggest the same with the best-selling 1960s albums of Allan Sherman and Mickey Katz, which would press Yinglish and middle-class Jewish obsessions into the mainstream, proving that you didn't have to be Jewish to appreciate Jewish humor. (As the title of the comedy album *You Don't Have to Be Jewish* in 1965, which gave Valerie Harper her first big break, urged.) All this stemming from—and in no small way contributing to—the increasing mainstream American acceptance of Judaism, with sociologists like Will Herberg positing a Jewish strand of American religiosity to stand co-equal, at least conceptually, with Catholicism and Protestantism (America's other religious traditions apparently not entering into the equation), and, in the wake of works like *Gentleman's Agreement*, the increasing sentiment that discrimination against the Jewish voice and body at least fell under the category of the lip service that vice pays to virtue.

And so the Jewish voice—led by Molly Goldberg on radio and television, by Sam Levenson, by Barth and Bruce, by Sherman and Katz, by *Mad*, by many others—was making its way into American households in the early to mid-1960s; and the arguments that jokes delivered in a Jewish accent were provincial were somewhat beside the point, because the country had begun to vote, with their wallets, to say that this particular kind of provincialism was all right with them. By 1966, after three albums, Brooks was finally able to say: "I did them because I wanted to do something for ethnic comedy . . . I wanted to leave something, because I'm spectacularly Jewish."[7] But that was six years later, when the question was settled. In 1960, with the question open, Brooks went into the recording studio with Reiner to cut 2,000 *Years with Carl Reiner and Mel Brooks.*

The nomenclatural order was only natural; Reiner was, of course, the incalculably bigger name back then, a lead on one of the biggest shows in American television history, a staple of talk shows and game shows, author of a well-received autobiographical novel, and on his way to becoming a successful television producer. Brooks was, to put it charitably, an industry name, and an only qualifiedly successful one at that. A brief squib on November 6, 1960, in the *Los Angeles Times* giving a roundup of recent releases—which included, in the same period, "a collection of [George] Jessel's work at testimonial dinners for assorted personalities" and a follow-up José Jiménez record—says the album "has the very talented Carl Reiner to insure some funny moments."[8]

The album was released on World Pacific, which at the time was best known for its cool jazz records. Lenny Bruce, more than anyone else, had solidified the link between jazz and comedy, with his hepcat talk and his play to the band ethos; but Brooks and Reiner were champions of the improvisational rhythms central to the form. The record jacket actually pointed out: "Bear in mind when listening to these routines that they are ad-libbed and that they are never the same twice," although what listeners actually heard on the albums, in fact, had been edited from several takes.[9] (Which allowed for more graceful conclusions. Once, at a party, Brooks couldn't think of a good capper to end one of the 2,000-Year-Old Man improv sessions, so he walked out mid-sentence, leaving behind only a note reading: "A Jew cries for help!")[10] The record sold a million copies, exhausting World Pacific's production capacity, and within several months the rights to the album for re-release had been sold to the larger Capitol Records for forty thousand dollars, a "highly unusual procedure," according to *Redbook*.[11] And before long the duo had produced a follow-up, 2,000 *and One Years with Carl Reiner & Mel Brooks*.[12]

But given Reiner and Brooks's high-profile connections, the rollout may have itself been unusually outsized. Within months of the fall premiere, by the end of January 1961, Brooks had sat down for an interview with Mike Wallace on Channel Thirteen; and less than two weeks later, Reiner and Brooks appeared on Ed Sullivan, doing their act alongside Henry Fonda's reading of Lincoln's Gettysburg address, songs by Peggy Lee and Paul Anka, and a modern dance "by the vivid Carmen de Lavallade."[13] And two days before the Wallace interview, the *Times* had included them in a roundup of recent comedy records. Admittedly, it was a mixed review, the critic finding the album "only intermittently funny . . . [with] an unconfined style pitched at a shouting level." But that was how he felt about all the records he reviewed, with one exception: Mike Nichols and Elaine May, he said, were "leading the league by far . . . as everyone knows, they are literate, satirical, and cuttingly observant."[14]

The "everyone knows" part is the key. Yes, Nichols and May's hugely successful theatrical twosome—taking off from the Chicago improvisational scene from whence came Shelley Berman as well—was an important influence. They were also the avatar of a certain kind of 1950s faux-intellectualism: though their act depended on the simulacrum of wit, name-dropping Pirandello and Albert Schweitzer, their audience didn't need to know much in order to follow what was going on; but they had to know, or feel smug about sort-of knowing, *something*. Part of Nichols and May's brilliance was to present the "everyone knows" conventional wisdom of the Manhattan sophisticate, polished to a high shine and reflected in a cracked, satirical mirror. Accordingly, their Jewishness was largely coded—May's hilarious, venom-tipped portrait of a Jewish mother in the skit "Mother and Son," reducing Nichols's rocket scientist to infantile goo in seven minutes of kvetching and twisting the Freudian knife, never mentions anything specific about religion or ethnicity.

Brooks and Reiner, of course, went the other way. In their discussion of Jewishness, of course, but also in their show-business conservatism. If the action in comedy was about the "sicknicks," the comedians who were topical, adventurous, satirical, taboo (but not too taboo; those unkosher comediennes like Barth and Pearl Williams were rarely if ever mentioned), Reiner and Brooks were old-school showbiz. They had an *act*. Not an "act," like Nichols and May; an *act*. And this was a certain kind of conservatism that would keep Brooks at arm's length from a certain kind of respectability among the hep, even as he sought to emulate and embrace it. Which may, in certain ways, have been good for his comedy, great for his bottom line, and necessary for his ego.

To start us off, take a possibly surprising departure point for a discussion of those first two 2,000-Year-Old Man albums, released so closely together they can be treated fairly uniformly. It's generally forgotten that the 2,000-Year-Old Man routine only covers about half the first album (the same is true for the second, by the way); the remainder is devoted to a variety of other skits, including a mini-suite of interviews that take place in that late 1950s/early '60s objective correlative for the new and vaguely suspiciously bohemian, the coffee house. Reiner's interviewer, seeking to investigate the denizens of this mysterious institution, encounters several characters played by Brooks: a depressed man (who, upon further research, turns out to be a woman), a Brando-esque actor (who introduces himself as a lesbian; "thespian," corrects Reiner), a painter (who offers to lacquer up his supper and sell it to Reiner for forty dollars), and, finally, a folk singer named Charlie Grape.

Grape is not particularly talented instrumentally (he plays "A"), or compositionally. When asked by Reiner to play one of his songs, he repeats the line, "22 men fell down and hurt their knee," several times; when asked for a new song, he sings the same song but changes the lyrics to "22 German soldiers hurt their knee." Finally, somewhere between bemused and frustrated, Reiner asks if Grape can do something topical. He is, after all, a folk singer—and, unspoken, he is also producing a comedy record in the age of topical satire. Grape thinks for a moment; and then comes up with: "Big Dick Nixon hurt his knee." The scene ends there, as the point is made: topicality, sophistication, are precisely not the point.

Neither is hipness, for that matter. Another of the non-2,000-Year-Old Man skits on the record, "Fabiola," flays the jazz hepcat, who, in response to Reiner's enthusing "you're dynamic! You're exciting!" mumbles, almost incoherently, "I've heard that, I've heard that" and refuses to know his own age: "I've got no time to look up who I am, what my life, my purpose . . . I don't know my life and my purpose. That's why I'm loved." In a sketch that could have come directly out of a *Your Show of Shows*, Brooks finally gets to take the role of his father figure Caesar by playing—appropriately enough—a psychologist. But Dr. Hall-Danish doesn't hold with the newfangled trends of analysis and Freud. He castigates his patients—"she spoke filthy," he says of one, "that girl is sick. She's nuts. Why do I have to hear that junk?" And his cures savor more of the old-school mentality of common sense, of *seykhel:* asked how he cured the young woman's obsessive habit of ripping paper, he replies: "I told her, don't tear paper. What? A nice girl like you? Don't tear paper." The point, then, is exactly the opposite from that of Nichols and May: the comic explosion of the expectation of such ambitions, in an unwillingness to identify with the new. Better, instead, to go back to the two thousand years old.

The first words we hear the 2,000-Year-Old Man speak—after, Reiner assures us, a six-day stay at the Mayo Clinic to recuperate from his journey to America from the Middle East—

are "oh, boy," a *krechtz* from the ages. But despite the gentleman's ostensible roots in the Middle East, and his uncanny memory for certain aspects of those early days—the fact that, for example, each cave had a national anthem, like, "let 'em all go to hell except Cave Seventy-Six!"—what he forgets is also indicative.

Less than five minutes into the first routine on the first album, Reiner asks what language they spoke back then. "Rock," the 2,000-Year-Old Man replies. "Basic rock . . . Two hundred years before Hebrew." Scenting comic possibility, Reiner digs deeper: "Do you *remember* your Hebrew, sir?" he asks. "Because I understand the modern Hebrew is different from the archaic." (Listeners might have paused, for a moment, to consider Paul Newman, whose presence as a modern Hebrew speaker—Ari Ben-Canaan in the film adaptation of Leon Uris's *Exodus*—had premiered within weeks of the release of Brooks and Reiner's album, and compared two very different-looking kinds of Jew.) Brooks rises to the challenge, or tries to:

> 2,000-YEAR-OLD MAN: The very ancient Hebrew is . . . [speaking in an even heavier accent, but simultaneously show-biz; shades of the variety comedian Marty Allen, even using his catchphrase] Uh, oh, hi dere. Hello. Hello dere. How are you . . .
>
> REINER: That's English!
>
> 2,000-YEAR-OLD MAN: Oh, vait, vait—
>
> REINER: Do you remember any Hebrew?
>
> 2,000-YEAR-OLD MAN: [laughing, trying not to break character] Very little, I think. Don't think I remember it . . . I must have forgotten a great deal of it. . . .
>
> REINER: I think you forgot it all, sir.
>
> 2,000-YEAR-OLD MAN: Maybe all, yes, maybe all. Thousands of years since I needed it.[15]

Brooks himself would later say that he'd attended Hebrew school—"shul, we called it. . . . We were the children of immigrants. . . . We faked it, nodded like we were praying. Learned enough Hebrew to get through our Bar Mitzvah. Hebrew is a very hard language for Jews."[16] Asked by Reiner if he'd ever had an accident in all this time, the Man, mishearing him, repeats: "an accent?"

The 2,000-Year-Old Man, then, with his origins at the Crucifixion, his recent arrival from the Middle East, and his linguistic and historical spottiness, is a peculiarly, if unsurprisingly, diasporic character, writ in a particularly American Jewish key. (Late in life, Brooks would describe the character, significantly, as "the Eastern European immigrant Jew, pronouncing himself forcefully, struggling to make it in America.") A brilliantly realized sequence in the album about the coming of Christianity to the Man's environs is transposed into the key of middle-class manufacturer: as a producer of Jewish stars, a low-price, high-cost item (it involved six men standing with points running at each other and hoping the thing would fuse together; there were "plenty of accidents"), the Man is given the opportunity by Simon (Peter) to switch over to crosses; only two men. Told it's going to be a "winning item that's gonna be a big seller," he nonetheless passes: "It's too simple," he recalls himself saying. "I didn't know it was *elokvent.*" His regrets, looking back, are commercial, not theological, and in the small-scale register of a *luftmensch:* "I woulda had over a 100 dollars today if I had a cross. They're in everywhere today."[17] He has more than forty-two thousand children and not one of them comes to visit, he complains, getting perhaps the hugest laugh of any joke in the routine from the live audience: not because it's revolutionary but because it's so familiar, the kind of line that had already become clichéd, just brilliantly reset. And not only in terms of framework, perhaps, but gender: here Brooks the old Jewish man becomes the archetypal Jewish mother. (Is it worth remembering the depressed man-turned-woman he plays later on the album? Possibly.)

The most audacious claim that Brooks and Reiner make on, and with, the Man, then, is not that American humor is

deeply Jewish. That was already well on its way to being established. It's that *everything* is. Robin Hood actually "stole from
everybody and kept everything"; thankfully, Marty the press agent
was right there on the spot to polish up his reputation.[18] And as
for William Shakespeare? Well, after a throwaway joke about
his writing—"Don't tell me he was a good writer. He had the
worst penmanship I ever saw in my life!"—Brooks recasts the
working playwright in the light of contemporary Broadway
mores. Informing Reiner that Shakespeare had written thirty-
eight plays, not thirty-seven as Reiner seems to think, he shares
the name of the lost play: Queen Alexandra and Murray. Reiner
asks him for a few lines of the play; after some pseudo-Elizabethan
garble from "Queen Alexandra," a typical Brooksian Jewish voice
responds: "Vat are you hollering? You'll wake up the whole cas-
tle." The Man is rueful: "This is a play that I invested money
in. . . . It closed in Egypt." Which anachronism gets a huge,
huge laugh.[19] As it did when they redid the bit on the Steve Allen
show in late 1961, where Brooks adds, after chiding the crowd,
"*Sha*, what noise!": "They shoulda made a musical out of it."
"Maybe you will someday," Reiner replies. This is probably not
the Rosetta stone to the last act of Brooks's career, but it does
provide interesting foreshadowing.

As did one other skit on the first album, a bit that runs less
than three minutes called simply "The Peruvian" in the track
list. Reiner tells us, speaking from "the jungles of Argentina,"
that "The Peruvian" is "a Spanish gentleman who owns a coffee plantation who calls himself Señor Lopez de Vega Diaz";
although we may be suspicious, first because Brooks's character
says, "yes, whatever . . . the name what we said, yes," and also
because he seems to be speaking in a German accent. Under
Reiner's questioning, the Peruvian falls apart, trying to cover
his misstatements ("Vee took Poland in nineteen days . . . NO!
the coffee beans can be matured in hothouses in nineteen days!";
"I vas only a sergeant in the Peruvian Indians!"). Finally, when

Reiner, with more bemusement than vitriol in his voice, conventions of the interview maintained, charges: "I don't believe you're Peruvian at all. I believe you're German, sir!" Brooks's choice is to drop bluster, to transform into a meek pussycat: "Vell, you found me out." Just six months before the album came out, David Ben-Gurion had announced the capture of Adolf Eichmann to the Knesset, and to the world; although Eichmann's trial, and thus the discussions of the banality of evil, were still in the future, Brooks had already begun to develop his artistic treatment of a subject that would occupy him for the rest of his career: attacking Nazis and Nazism through minimization and ridicule.

Brooks and Reiner, recall, had linked their original reticence to making the 2,000-Year-Old Man public directly to Nazism and the Holocaust. Was their comfort with including "The Peruvian"—with doing the 2,000-Year-Old Man more generally—also linked to an increasing comfort with discussing the war against the Jews? Does this speak to another blow to the theory that "no one talked about the Holocaust" in these early postwar years?

Maybe so, maybe not, as the Man might have said. It's certainly the case that this kind of humor was around back then, if you knew where to look. You didn't even need to look very hard, not with Lenny Bruce holding up a newspaper with a fake headline reading SIX MILLION JEWS FOUND ALIVE IN ARGENTINA. But there's a difference between Bruce's treatment and Brooks and Reiner's: the former is a Jewish joke, a Holocaust joke. The latter is a joke about Nazis. And as the former member of the 1104th Engineer Combat Group could certainly tell you, there were a lot of ex-GIs out there, or who were no longer out there, with wives, family members, friends, a lot of Americans, who were perfectly capable of hating Nazis even if they didn't happen to be Jewish, and infuriated that some of them seemed to have escaped justice to live comfortable lives in certain South American countries, and were happy to see someone take them on. Ironically, Brooks's anti-Nazi humor would require the infusion of other elements to become part of his contribution to the Jewish comedy canon.

"I wanna tell ya, it's been a wonderful 2,000 years and you've been a wonderful civilization," is the Man's signoff at the end of the first album's routine.[20] It was the kind of showbizzy line that could have been spoken on a Vegas stage, or at an awards show. And they almost got the chance: in addition to selling those million copies, 2,000 *Years with Carl Reiner and Mel Brooks* was nominated for a Grammy award in the spoken comedy category for 1961.[21] Comedy had only been recognized as a Grammy category since 1959, bespeaking the new interest in recorded comedy: but it had followed, and reflected, the changing, increasingly Jewish nature of American comedy. The list of Jewish nominees between 1959 and 1962 alone included Elaine May and Mike Nichols, Mort Sahl (twice), Betty Comden and Adolph Green, Bernie Green, Lenny Bruce, Shelley Berman (a winner, and then a subsequent nominee), and Tom Lehrer.

Brooks and Reiner lost. Not to Nichols and May, whose seminal album would be nominated (and win) the following year, but to Bob Newhart's *The Button-Down Mind Strikes Back!*, whose predecessor, *The Button-Down Mind of Bob Newhart*, was in some ways the revolutionary album that had kickstarted the comedy record boom in the first place. (To give you a sense of its seismic impact, it won Album of the Year at the Grammys, beating out Harry Belafonte, Frank Sinatra, and Nat King Cole. Newhart won best New Artist as well.) In October 1961, the week before Brooks and Reiner appeared on the Steve Allen show to promote the second 2,000-Year-Old Man album, Newhart debuted in his own television show.[22] But even if Brooks wasn't the hottest comedy star of the moment, he was on his way to becoming a genuine bold-faced name, even if in tandem with another, more famous face. In an interview in 1967, Carl

Reiner would say, "Mel Brooks used to be very depressed. He used to go around saying, 'Hello, I'm Mel Brooks. I wrote the Sid Caesar show.' But becoming a performer made him feel better."[23]

And things were looking up in his personal life as well: on February 5, 1961, Brooks went to the Ziegfeld Theater to meet his future wife.

The theater was hosting rehearsals for the Perry Como variety show *Kraft Music Hall,* and the actress Anne Bancroft was going over her number for the program. The song was a fairly new composition—it had been part of a recently expanded version of an extended musical suite called *Manhattan Tower,* by Gordon Jenkins, about a romance that takes place in the apartment building of the same name. "Married I Can Always Get" began by describing the connubial state as "not my cup of tea, they won't throw rice at me for a while yet!" and continued in a similar vein, with the singer insisting she'll live the life she's used to, "get a ring when I choose to." And Bancroft, the former Anna Maria Louisa Italiano, knew whereof she sung.

She knew she could get married; she'd already been—to an attorney, when she was in her early twenties, a four-year starter marriage that was finally dissolved as her acting career was beginning to skyrocket, after a promising start that was followed by a period of limbo. Although she'd done movies and television early on, her recent momentum had come in the theater: she'd won back-to-back Tonys in 1958 and 1959, the first for a featured role as Gittel Mosca, a Jewish dancer from the Bronx, alongside Henry Fonda in *Two for the Seesaw,* and the second, far more famously, as Helen Keller's teacher Annie Sullivan in *The Miracle Worker.* In an era when Broadway was, even with television's recent inroads, far closer to the heart of the culture than today, she was, in every way, a star. Brooks was, to put it mildly, not intimidated; the moment she finished her song he ran forward, applauding, and introduced himself: "I'm Mel Brooks. Hiya, A."[24]

What was Brooks doing there in the first place? Although all the accounts agree that the story did happen, that doesn't mean there wasn't a story behind the story. Some suggest it was a setup through a mutual friend; others that the meeting started as an "agency package," presumably to couple up the troublingly liberated Ms. Bancroft for public consumption. If so, the odds were no one actually expected much of it—Bancroft didn't pick that song out of thin air, after all; and Brooks, who at almost exactly the same time as the Ziegfeld meeting was being hauled into court for failure to pay alimony, hearing, once more, charges of adultery and abuse leveled against him, presumably shared the attitude expressed in the title of the unproduced, quasi-autobiographical screenplay he would soon begin work on: *Marriage Is a Dirty Rotten Fraud.*[25]

But what Bancroft hadn't counted on was being bowled over by the writer's energy, joy, and hilarity; expressing, within the confines of a relationship, the same ethos of unconventionality she was singing about. For his part, Brooks felt the same; with the addition, not incidentally, of basking in the knowledge that he was desired, and desirable, by the object of others' celebration. Brooks had always considered himself physically second-rate next to his professional partners—and not just the leonine Caesar. In one of the skits on *2,000 Years with Carl Reiner and Mel Brooks,* purporting to be an astronaut, Brooks claims that the extremely handsome pioneers of space everyone knows are "models," so that America won't be embarrassed to show off their crews in front of Russia. Reiner nods: "You're not a very good-looking man." "No, I'm a monkey," Brooks responds immediately, and as much as he's in on the joke, the laughter couldn't have helped stinging a bit. This man—who couldn't *possibly* be an astronaut, a cowboy, a front-of-camera talent, except as a comedian, a twisted jokey version of the star—he could *catch* one.

It was noted that long after they were married in August 1964, Brooks kept up the habit of referring to his wife in professional situations by her full name, as "Anne Bancroft."[26] And, although of course Bancroft wasn't Jewish, that didn't matter to Brooks. Their marriage finally took place the same year as *Fiddler on the Roof* premiered, a play that put the question of interfaith marriage front and center, framing it—in archetypal postwar fashion—as a challenge of liberal values of the individual over the potentially invidious divisiveness of tradition, the shtetl's commitment to everyone keeping to their own circumscribed role precluding the possibility of like minds and souls meeting. (The fact that *Fiddler*, unlike the stories it's based on, ends by looking from a vanishing shtetl toward America says a lot about its hierarchies of value.)[27] But Brooks's rationale for going forward with an interfaith marriage was quite different. "She don't need to convert," he would say at the time. "She's a star!"[28]

Which also says a lot, especially considering that just a few years earlier an unquestionably bigger star, Elizabeth Taylor, had indeed converted to Judaism, to marry Eddie Fisher. So there was precedent. But Brooks's Judaism, so deeply important to him, was never invested in the theological. If there was a religious faith to him, it was in show business. And of course, like *Fiddler*, he was reflecting a trend. Between 1961 and 1966, a little less than a sixth of American Jews who got married were marrying Gentiles; that number was quadruple pre-1960 figures—and half of what it would be between 1966 and 1972.[29] As was often his wont, Brooks turned one of the central dilemmas of the situation—what to tell the parents—into a joke; on the David Susskind show, he claimed that when he told his mother he was bringing Bancroft over to meet her, she replied: "That's fine. I'll be in the kitchen; my head'll be in the oven."[30]

The idea of the unlikely Jew turned American hero—or, at least, right next door to it—was percolating in Brooks's professional life, too. About two weeks before he met Bancroft for the first time, he had gotten what seemed to be another big

Broadway break. The producers of the enormous hit *Bye Bye Birdie*, Edward Padula and L. Slade Brown, signed Brooks to adapt the Pulitzer Prize winner Robert Lewis Taylor's *Professor Fodorski* to the stage as a musical under the title *All-American*, complementing *Birdie*'s music and lyrics team, Charles Strouse and Lee Adams.[31] (Brooks had almost certainly gotten the nod through *Birdie* book writer and *Caesar's Hour* alum Michael Stewart, who'd left the team to write *Carnival!*)

Taylor had written his comic novel about a Hungarian émigré professor who uses his scientific engineering methods at the (nonexistent) Southern Baptist Institute of Technology to teach football—and vice versa. In the novel, published in 1950, the protagonist is clearly if obliquely Jewish—he has a cousin Hillel, and the objections to his appointment as temporary coach of the football team, despite his odd success at football, are in part clearly rooted in hostility to his religion, coded by references to his refugee status. "He's, ah, shall we say, a refugee, from an undesirable element of Europe," a member of the college's board says. "This is a Christian college, devoted to certain ideals of conduct and philosophy. His appointment would be most inappropriate."[32] Conversely, Fodorski's embrace of football and the collegiate spirit are, in some way, clear metaphors for the Jew embracing—and complexly being embraced by— America. "We're going to make it a love letter, a funny love letter, to America," the producer Edward Padula said about the show.[33] (One of the musical numbers was called "The Old Immigration and Naturalization Rag," with lines like: "Put us in/Your big American Melting Pot and/Melt us! Melt us!")[34]

If this seemed a bit, well, ethnic for American audiences— this was still a few years before *Fiddler*, remember—that was easy enough to water down even further in the adaptation. Given the subject matter, there was athleticism aplenty—especially once the director Joshua Logan, who'd shared his own Pulitzer with Rodgers and Hammerstein for *South Pacific* and had a list of credits to make the jaw drop and the mouth water—came on board.[35] Logan provided locker-room scenes for audiences to ogle at, "fill[ing] the stage with well-built men bare to the waist. In the number 'Physical Fitness,' fifteen gypsies formed a four-tiered human pyramid while extolling the joys of getting in shape; the cast album liner notes explain, 'The stripped-down athletes may be wretched football players, but they have glorious muscles, and prove it athletically.'"[36]

A variety of people who knew Logan, not least Jane Fonda, have claimed he was a closeted gay man, and whether or not the homoerotic subtext of *All-American* was intentional—it seems hard to believe it wasn't—it's not impossible to see the scene pictures as enjoyed and encouraged, even if not created, by Brooks as an early turn in his love of spectacle toward camp. (Susan Sontag's "Notes on Camp" was published in 1964.) But whatever else it was, it seemed destined to be a sure hit. So certain were people, in fact, that producers of *Birdie* were baying to get in on the action. The *Times* dryly summarized: "It is understood Columbia Records wanted to put up the entire backing for 'All American.' In view of the support given by the loyal backers of 'Bye Bye Birdie,' Columbia was prevailed upon to reduce its stake to 50 percent or $200,000."[37]

But what was obvious to all doesn't always prove to be the case, not when it comes to the theater. Logan vetoed everyone else's choice for the lead, Zero Mostel, who was battling his way back from the HUAC blacklist and beginning to return to theatrical stardom; instead the director went with an old working partner, Ray Bolger, whom he'd directed in the huge success *Where's Charley?* in 1948.[38] Bolger was signed for two years, in a return to Broadway after a decade's absence. Trial performances were to start in January in Detroit, then Philadelphia, with a "flexible New York opening date" of February 21, 26, or

March 1, 1962.[39] The date was then moved to March 19—never a good sign.[40] And it wasn't: Brooks, it's said, never got around to writing the second act; and the resulting pieced-together work—where "Fodorski's new fame was exploited by Madison Avenue, by 1962 too well worn a satirical target," according to Ken Mandelbaum—lasted just eighty-six performances.[41]

Bolger was universally lambasted as miscast; the *Times* called Brooks's efforts "diffuse and heavy-handed," and *Newsweek* said his "libretto bites off much that it should eschew."[42] The backers all lost their shirts; and Brooks was left, perhaps, with the image of baying producers trying to put their money into a hit that turned into a flop, one of Broadway's more infamous. How would the story go, he might have wondered, if the same thing happened—but on purpose? It was as *All-American* was about to enter its out-of-town tryouts, after all, that the show's producer Padula acquired a new comedy by Brooks. This one was tentatively called *Springtime for Hitler.*

It had started as a comic novel. Why not? Everyone was doing it; his comedic partner Carl Reiner had written a fairly sensitive and quasi-autobiographical one, *Enter Laughing*, that had gotten respectful reviews and was about to be adapted into a play. (It premiered in 1963, won Alan Arkin a Tony, and marked the directing debut of the Broadway legend Gene Saks.) Brooks's métier, on the other hand, was not the fine brush of personal introspection; instead, he went back to one of his long-term idées fixes: Nazis. And making fun of them. But his antic nature, his *shpilkes*, made him unsuited for the contemplative hours in the novelist's chair; he preferred performing his bits, acting them out, even if others would eventually bring them to life. And that would be the case here; the métier seemed quite different from Brooks's regular stomping grounds. Padula reported that "actually 'Hitler is not in the comedy.' 'It's a sort of a play-within-a-play. The setting is contemporary England.'" Under consideration for the leading role: Kenneth Williams,

"England's new comic discovery."[43] The *Times* also reported that the play would be produced the following season.[44]

Whether it was because of the financial disaster of their partnership on *All-American*, disillusionment with Brooks's work on the project, or simply that he never finished the play, *Springtime* obviously did not appear on Broadway the following year. Or possibly it was thanks to a conversation he had while serving as a script doctor on a Broadway production. Brooks did this on multiple occasions: in an in-depth look at the musical *Kelly*, which opened and closed the same night in February 1965, Lewis Lapham described Brooks and another TV writer brought in to a troubled David Susskind production at the eleventh hour. "A small, energetic man with thinning hair," in Lapham's description, Brooks gives firm, confident advice in typically colorful locution: "The first three numbers in Act Two are the worst, seventy-five miles an hour into a stone wall. Death. Three numbers back to back."[45] The two rewrote the show substantially; but the actors' concerns about "Jewish nightclub humor" lines like "You can't welsh on an Englishman," "Why don't you English on a Welshman?" were, it seemed, well warranted: the notices were "ruinous."[46]

But this exchange occured during an earlier gig, on yet *another* Broadway flop, *Nowhere to Go but Up*, a musical about "celebrated Prohibition agents Izzy Einstein and Moe Smith, known for their integrity and clever disguises," directed by the American Jewish auteur Sidney Lumet—already known as a distinguished director for television and his *Twelve Angry Men*, but less well known for his comic touch, and even less for his musical chops. *Nowhere to Go but Up* was the last time he appeared on Broadway; and the last musical he turned his hand to until *The Wiz* in 1978. The show opened in the fall of 1962 and closed after a week. Brooks was doubly lucky, though. First, he wasn't credited; and second, the show's producer, Kermit Bloomgarden, whom Brooks had accosted decades earlier pretending to

be Paul Muni, heard his *Springtime* pitch and told him in no un-
certain terms that, with thirty-three scenes and fifty-five actors,
Springtime for Hitler wasn't a play. It was a film.[47]

Brooks's other efforts to work with the cream of the new
postwar American Jewish crop of artists were also meeting with
little success. A television pilot for Zero Mostel, now fresh off
his triumph in *A Funny Thing Happened on the Way to the Forum*,
in which Mostel would play a janitor with dreams of artistic
success, was dismissed by the actor as "creatively worthless."
This notwithstanding a developing robust friendship between
the two; along with canonical American Jewish author Joseph
Heller and several others, including, eventually, the *Godfather*
author Mario Puzo, they would go out for cheap Chinese food
every Tuesday night. The Group of the Oblong Table, they
called themselves, a nod to both Knights of the Round and Algonquin: "I'm sure we're funnier than the Algonquin crowd,
but we're not as bright," Brooks would say.

Brooks also tried to adapt William Steig's 1953 book *Dreams
of Glory and Other Drawings*, about a kid's fantasies. Possibly
taking a page from what had happened to Reiner's show—by
1962, the Gentile version of Reiner's life had reached top ten
in the ratings; by the next year it was in the top three—Brooks
turned the child protagonist into a twelve-year-old Brooklyn
non-Jew and called the show *Inside Danny Baker*. It didn't go
anywhere.[48] Even his fallback, working for Caesar, was losing
not only its burnish but its sense of possibility: critics hated
As Caesar Sees It, the Sunday night half-hour Brooks was head
writer on. Yes, there were the late night talk show appearances—
he was on the premiere episode of *The Tonight Show with Johnny
Carson*—which helped raise his profile (and the appearance fees
helped, and he needed the money, three hundred and twenty
dollars for a *Tonight Show* appearance), but a higher profile for
spitballing jokes on guest couches wasn't the same as professional *success*.[49]

Yes, by any normal standard, Brooks was remarkably successful, Emmy and Grammy nominated; but he was living with a Tony and Oscar winner. (Bancroft had won the Oscar for reprising her role as Annie Sullivan in *The Miracle Worker*'s film version.) Was there professional jealousy there? Did he bridle at the tone in which he was dismissed in some Bancroft profiles—"She hopes to marry Mel Brooks, an American writer, this summer, but this does not mean the end of her career"—or patronized in other news items?[50] "Anne Bancroft's boyfriend, writer Mel Brooks, will head for London to be with her for her Sept. 17 birthday. Mel, who has made a big name on his own via his 2,000-year-old man character, may well make Anne his bride in the near future if the romance continues on its present happy course."[51] There was a notice in December about postponing their wedding plans, which may have been because they were "both too busy to take time off for the long honeymoon they want."[52] Or, possibly, as Bancroft had said a month earlier in announcing the wedding would take place the following spring, that "Mel and I realize we would have to base our marriage on the motto, 'Career comes last'. . . . At the moment, you might say we're stalling. We know that love isn't enough."[53] When they eventually did get married, at the city clerk's office on August 5, 1964, one account said that only a few weeks before, "Mel spent an hour trying to explain to a buddy why he didn't believe in marriage."[54]

The notices in the leading papers didn't even mention Brooks's name in the headline. "Anne Bancroft, Comedy Writer Married in N.Y.," the *Los Angeles Times* noted; the *New York Times* went with "Comedian Weds Anne Bancroft."[55] In New York, Brooks was simply a "comedy writer and comedian"; the paper of record in the industry city, though, did note that "both are movie academy award winners." Because in the interim, Brooks had managed to at least match Bancroft on the mantel in one respect—and he did it by going back and doubling down on what worked best for him: looking at other material and throwing spitballs at it from the back seats.

Conservative spitballs, we might say. If the new fronts of American popular culture were a riot of shape and color, symbolized by the trends in abstract expressionism and "modern art," it was still taking its time to sift its way down to the mass medium in which Brooks had done much of his visual work so far. Although the first national color TV broadcast had been in 1954 (the Tournament of Roses Parade), a decade later only three percent of American households had color sets, and the majority of network television programs didn't appear in color until 1965. And in some ways it was more natural to Brooks, looking at this artistic leading edge, to take a position standing athwart it and yelling stop. Or, more precisely, "Vhat d'ell is this?" These are the words of the voice-over narrator in *The Critic*, the Oscar-winning short animated film written and narrated by Brooks. Made in 1963, around the time Roy Lichtenstein and Robert Rauschenberg were beginning to make their marks, it's available on YouTube. It's only three minutes and twenty-five seconds long. Go watch it. We'll wait.[56]

Brooks had certainly been aware of the animator and filmmaker Ernest Pintoff's work as early as 1959, when Carl Reiner had provided all the voices for an earlier Oscar-nominated short cartoon, *The Violinist*.[57] In a little over seven minutes, Pintoff took viewers through an examination of one of the enduring questions of aesthetics: how much does one need to suffer for one's art? The protagonist, who as our story opens plays with technical proficiency but "no feeling," consults the brilliant Professor Fillinger, who, in classic Caesar Germanesque, informs him: "to play with feeling one must zuffer. Zuffer, zuffer." And so he does, sacrificing pleasure and, indeed, personal hygiene to his art: upon returning to Professor Fillinger, having neither shaved nor cut his hair in a very long time, the latter moans: "Ooh, that's too much suffering! . . . Get me a bowl of chicken soup, I'm suffering from too much suffering!" And so the violinist, chastened, rejects the pursuit of Art for the pursuit of Normality: "Harry was no genius," Reiner sums up. "On the contrary, Harry was quite normal."

There's certainly some satirical sensibility there—Harry's normal involves eating bear meat on the subway—but one is left with the sense that Pintoff and Reiner's ambit is the zany but not the strange; that Harry's genius—which was, it seems, achievable—is too high a price to pay for art; that being embraced by society (at film's end, Harry finds a personal connection with a potential romantic partner) wins out over the potentially alienating pursuit of revolutionary artistic transformation. A lot to put on a short cartoon; but the ethos, 1950s-forged, was essential to Reiner and Brooks's sensibility.

Which became even clearer in *The Critic*, in which Brooks showed that the rejection of that model of revolutionary, alienating genius could also bear its own genius within it. Pintoff designed the film as "a spoof of the pseudo-art film" that could serve as a curtain-raiser for full-length features. For his part, Brooks claimed to be inspired by an old immigrant man complaining at the back of one of those shorts, an experimental film by Norman McLaren. "Don't let me see the images in advance," he told Pintoff. "Just let them assault me."[58] And the combination of parody and fealty created a kind of manifesto.

The visuals are sweet and lovely: pictures of geometrical shapes changing form and color in time to baroque music. But then comes the voice. "This is cute, this is cute, this is nice. Vat da hell is it?" Although it's accented, it's not the 2,000-Year-Old Man's voice. It's a little deeper, a little more aggrieved; it's every father Philip Roth is writing about in *Goodbye, Columbus*, every first-generation American Jewish man looking with horror at the intellectual exercises his children are wasting his money on in some expensive liberal arts college: "It must be some symbolism . . . I think it's symbolic of junk." Occasionally, there are attempts to shush him, but the critic remains undeterred. "That fella that made this . . . Vat does he vaste his time with this? A fella like that, he probably could drive a truck, do something constructive. Make a shoe." "I don't know much about psychanalysis," he concludes, "but I'd say this is a dirty picture."

That's critics for you, goes the punchline: intellectual types who read sex into everything, Freudians to a one. "This cartoon will evoke a joyful response in the hearts of many who have experienced the host of post-, sub-, pseudo-, and neo-McLaren abstract cartoon films," wrote (believe it or not) *Critic* magazine, and although Brooks may be less sanguine about McLaren than the anonymous reviewer, he understood, more fully, what his role was.[59] Around the same time Brooks was receiving the Oscar, he wrote a TV sketch for Zero Mostel, "The Actor Prepares," in which "Zero, as the flamboyant performer, went through the hell of stage fright and insecurity before stepping onto the stage to be hit by a custard pie."[60] The Method—the doubling down on performance as Art—gives way to the joyful response of just getting a good old vaudevillian pie in the face, that explosive deflation of pretense. Others saw Brooks as emblematic of this bandwagon early on. Writing a letter of comment to the *Times* on "Notes on Cult," a Victor Navasky article about Norman Podhoretz and his circle, his friend Joseph Heller observed: "If brilliance is to be a criterion, there is more in . . . three minutes with Mel Brooks . . . than is apt to be found in a three-year subscription to Commentary." (Heller would later say the protagonist of his 1979 novel *Good As Gold*, a short Jewish man, had "a great deal of Mel" in him.)[61]

Of course, it should be noted that it's the Critic who makes the connection to sex; and though Brooks may not be interested in all the pretentiousness, he sure gets the idea of subtext. Which bespeaks an intellectualism we'll return to. Brooks would continue, after *The Critic*'s success, to release movie trailers and radio and television spots for forthcoming movies. Some were rejected by exhibitors; the reason, according to *Variety*, was that they were "too New Yorkish," which may be a fairly transparent euphemism for "too Jewish," but may also, simultaneously, suggest that as much as Brooks wants to be loved by the crowd, his sensibility isn't—entirely—of it.[62] Working out that push and pull became the task of Brooks's 1960s.

About a week after that Mostel sketch aired, Brooks appeared on another episode of David Susskind's *Open End*—this one called "Strictly for Laughs," featuring Nipsey Russell and Bill Cosby among others.[63] Within a month, Susskind's partner Daniel Melnick had pitched a new television show he was packaging to Brooks. Melnick's pitch was James Bond meets Inspector Clouseau; by the time Brooks was talking it up to the trade magazines, he was describing it as "a touch of James Bond and a lot of Mel Brooks."[64] Part of that was Brooks trying to raise his profile, of course; but the difference between the French Clouseau (played to perfection by the British comedy icon Peter Sellers in 1963's *The Pink Panther* and *A Shot in the Dark*, which hit theaters a month after Brooks made his remark in 1964) and the American Jewish Brooks spoke volumes, too.

James Bond predated the British invasion; his explosion onto American bedside tables actually came as a result of a book recommendation by President John F. Kennedy. But Bond, and Kennedy, were the antithesis of *yiddishe* humor—if Mort Sahl could make Ike jokes, saying that he was out of it, a hopelessly unhep goyishe golfer, it was much harder to make the same kinds of claims about Kennedy. You couldn't even call him the most deadly thing you could call a Gentile—unfunny—since the Kennedy wit, to take one of the titles of the numberless hagiographic books about him, was legendary. (And still holds up: his line about being the man who escorted Jackie Kennedy to Paris is still a great opener.) Bond himself was known—especially in his cinematic incarnation, then portrayed by Sean Connery—for a kind of icy, debonair wit. This was not the type of comedy that Brooks's new show, *Get Smart*, would traffic in.

"He's no Sean Connery or Gregory Peck. He's just an ordinary guy with a hero's job," said Don Adams, who played the show's lead character, Maxwell Smart.[65] But Adams's natural desire to frame himself as an American Everyman notwithstanding, that isn't quite right.[66] For Brooks, the way to produce an American parody—a Brooksian American parody—was to turn him into a bit of a, well, a *schlemiel*. "No one had ever done a show about an idiot before," Brooks told *Time* magazine in 1965. "I decided to be the first."[67] And it's true: Maxwell Smart, despite often saving the day, is at heart an ode to failure. And the particular kind of failure Smart exudes—I'd like to suggest—is not only Jewish, but theatrical.

Watch that classic opening to *Get Smart* again, the one with all the jaunty music. Smart basically walks through a series of opening curtains, in order to take his turn on the stage, and in the spotlight. And then he fails; or, in failing, succeeds (and don't think *that* pattern doesn't recur—and isn't it a pattern, we might say at the risk of sounding a little too Jewishly exegetical, that historians could seize on to characterize the entire history of the Jewish diaspora?). And in doing so, he also seems to undergo every actor's nightmare. The scenes that everyone remembers from *Get Smart*—the best scenes—are the set pieces that come straight out of shows gone wrong: the mispronunciations, not getting the tech to work right. In the first moments of the pilot episode, which aired on September 18, 1965, Smart leaves his seat at the symphony to take a call from the Chief on his shoe phone and locks himself in the janitor's closet he's ducked into for secrecy. What opening night in the theater doesn't include the fear of a sticking stage door?

Smart, his name notwithstanding, is hardly the sharpest tool in the box. (If this irony seems cheap to you, here's a reminder that the head of the evil spy agency KAOS, Mr. Big, is played by a little person—a not uncharacteristically unsubtle joke.) He fails strategically; he fails operationally; he fails bureaucratically. There's a reason that "Sorry about that, Chief," became a byword; Smart kept doing things he needed to apologize for. And he wasn't only uncool, he was unhip, a suit and tux man in an increasingly bell-bottomed world. The climax of the second episode—in which *Get Smart*, as if it knew it was symbolically meaningful, changes from the pilot's black and white to color—revolves in no small part around Smart's inability to do any of the new, modern go-go dances like the Watusi or the Pony. (Watching people do it, he believes they may be under some kind of KAOS influence.)

Smart even fails rhetorically, perhaps his most essential failure—both as an actor and as a (metaphorical) Jew. His constant refrain of "Would you believe . . . ," with the constant deflationary response of disbelief, which then leads him to revise and ultimately diminish his claims to absurdity, shows that he can't persuade people of who and what he claims to be and have. Which is another way to say: he can't pass. As an actor; as a spy; as an ultra-cool Gentile. It just doesn't work for him. Compare this to the other spy shows of the time, the non-parodic ones. *The Man from U.N.C.L.E.* (which premiered the year before *Get Smart*, in September 1964) and *Mission: Impossible* (which appeared the year after, in September 1966) constantly involve disguise and acting—an essential tool of spycraft, to be sure—and generally involve our identification with the actor-spies as successful actors.

And in *I Spy*, the hugely successful show featuring Mel Brooks's co-panelist Bill Cosby—which premiered literally three days before *Get Smart*—it's Cosby who pulls off the high-wire act: not only playing a spy, but acting as part of an integrated cast and scenario, if not in society. (And with remarkable success; Cosby won three Emmys in three years for the role.) It's something Maxwell Smart never manages to do. He's too loud, too outside, too much himself, to actually pass. Constantly tripping and smashing over stuff, he's as subtle as a bull in a china shop—or a Jew, at least a Jew of Brooks's mien, in a country club. This era was the high-water mark of the country club joke, of the Jew trying to put on an act and never managing to pull it off. Those Jews in the jokes who almost make it through the final initiation dinner and then shout "oy vey!" when the soup gets spilled on them—what are they doing but failing to maintain their cover stories? It's true, Maxwell Smart may be working for CONTROL. But it's not a good fit. What he needs—what makes him work—is KAOS.

Some of the reviews were mixed—the reviewer in the *Times*, for example, suggested that "the use of a dwarf in the part of 'Mr. Big' was indicative of an undercurrent of tastelessness," but conceded that with "a massive dose of restraint, however, 'Get Smart!' might still make it."[68] It did. Brooks and his co-creator Buck Henry earned Emmy nominations for both the pilot and the series, losing to *The Dick Van Dyke Show* for both, as did Don Adams; but the show went on to run for five years, and in its first year it was the second-highest rated show on NBC, just behind *Bonanza*.[69]

Maxwell Smart, and the show that bore his name, wasn't only Brooks, of course. Not by a long shot. Melnick had pitched the idea to Brooks and Buck Henry, né Henry Zuckerman, under the working title "Super Spy." Don Adams, whose father was a Hungarian Jew, came up with the "Would you believe . . ." gag, along with the catch-phrase "Sorry about that."[70] Brooks came up with the title and the lead character's name (using his father's name); and this, along with Brooks's leverage, led to a "Created by Mel Brooks" credit in the deal memo, although by the time it aired, the credit had been changed to "Created by Mel Brooks with Buck Henry." More than fitting, considering the comparative work the two put in on the show; even before it aired, Henry was doing the job of talking it up to the *Los Angeles Times*, and several months later a press report said that while the show "blithely continues to climb the rating charts, there is a tremendous war going on behind the scenes. Writer Mel Brooks, who was hired to assist in the development of the original idea, which he shared, hasn't been around in four months—with the exception of dropping in to meet with a magazine interviewer—and the rest of the staff is furious."[71]

Brooks's attention had been divided. He'd been trying to land a writer-director deal at Universal for a picture starring Bancroft, according to Dorothy Kilgallen; and in the summer and fall of that year there were stories floated in the papers, then retracted or denied, of a pregnancy.[72] By the month after *Get Smart* premiered, Bancroft, denying reports to Hedda Hopper that "she was unhappy in her marriage to Mel Brooks," also said, answering why Brooks wasn't writing for her, that "he is the type who has to write what he has to, and cannot write just for her." "Being married to Mel Brooks is wonderful work," she said several months later. "He has lots of temperament. I'm a temperamental actress. It means I have to harness a bit of my own temperament."[73]

In her interview with Hopper, Bancroft said she was coming east; he was staying in Los Angeles, she said, to work on *Get Smart* and a movie script. Although he didn't seem to be working very actively on the television show, he certainly was working: writing gags for Andy Williams and Johnny Carson's Timex specials, and, more famously, a series of Young & Rubicam spots for Ballantine Beer where the "spectacularly Gentile" Dick Cavett (in Brooks's words) interviewed a "2,500-Year-Old Brewmaster" who came up, improvisationally, with lines like "my tongue just threw a party for my mouth." The ad exec Alex Kroll said: "You can put a thousand copywriters down in front of a thousand typewriters for a thousand years and never come up with that line. That's why you have a Mel Brooks, because he can give you that flash of genius."[74]

That said, despite the critical raves, the commercial appeal apparently didn't follow—at least, that was the reason the *Times* suggested for why Ballantine pulled the account from Young & Rubicam within months. "This is not the first time that Young & Rubicam has created a comedy hit in the reviews here, if not in the box office," the paper reported, another indication, like in the wake of *The Critic*, that Brooks's comic sensibility might not have the mass appeal he'd hoped for.[75] In an interview with the *Los Angeles Times*—maybe even the interview the *Get Smart* team was furious about—Brooks identified his own sensibility with Main Street's: "We were really satisfying our own tastes. Could we then satisfy everybody, reach the little towns? The answer was basic. 'Funny' was the common denominator."[76] But ultimately Brooks, though foundational to *Get Smart*'s template, was less involved with its ongoing commercial success. And the movie script Bancroft was presumably alluding to would take this dichotomy to its height.

A movie called, at the time, *Springtime for Hitler.*

Literally the night before *Get Smart* premiered, CBS had debuted *Hogan's Heroes*, a sitcom set in a German prisoner of war camp, and one of the most important cultural vectors for the over-the-top Nazi accent in the person of Colonel Wilhelm Klink. American mass culture had been making fun of Nazi accents since the 1930s; you couldn't pick up a wartime comic book without seeing a couple. *Hogan's Heroes* itself, set in Stalag 13, owes its cultural resonance to the 1951 comedy-drama *Stalag 17*, directed by Billy Wilder, which was itself based on a Broadway play of the same name. And speaking of show business: Lenny Bruce famously did bits about Hitler and show business, including a Hitler Musical, and *he* was almost certainly influenced by the comic Will Jordan, who'd done a routine about showbiz types casting a replacement for Hitler. This to say nothing of the wartime mockery of Hitler and the Nazis, ranging from Jack Benny's brilliant *To Be or Not to Be* to the off-color songs mocking Hitler and company's sexual failings.

All this made the mainstream a little uneasy. Jack Gould, writing in the *Times*, took on "the depiction of the Nazis as silly old buffoons . . . hopeless oafs having more in common with Desilu Studios than Hitler. There's something a little sick about 'Hogan's Heroes,' an insensitive and misguided extension of Hollywood television's all too prevalent belief that anything and everything can be converted into cheap slapstick."[77] But when it came to Brooks, Gould had it wrong: this kind of comedy was dearly bought indeed.

As Brooks put it a few years later, somewhat pungently: "Me? Not like the Germans? Why should I not like Germans? Just because they're arrogant and have fat necks and do anything they're told as long as it's cruel, and killed millions of Jews in concentration camps and made soap out of their bodies and lamp shades out of their skins? Is that any reason to hate their fucking guts?"[78] For him, Nazism was a scourge, "the great outrage of the twentieth century. There is nothing to compare with it. And . . . so what can I do about it? If I get on the soapbox and wax eloquently it'll be blown away in the wind, but if I do *Springtime for Hitler* it'll never be forgotten. I think you can bring down totalitarian governments faster by using ridicule than you can with invective."

And so ridicule it was. In a third 2,000-Year-Old Man album, *Carl Reiner and Mel Brooks at the Cannes Film Festival*, released in 1962, Brooks plays one "Adolph Hartler" at the "Narzi Film Festival" who flails in the manner of the earlier album's Peruvian, but here the humor is significantly more pointed. "Hitler made some terrible errors," says the man who explains his SS tattoo as stemming from his captaincy of the Simon Says team. "Like losing the war." He even hid a Jewish family "in our own home—hid them, and then turned them over." Brooks's comic novel, for its part, had revolved around a poor, misunderstood Viennese youth named Adolf, and how all he wanted to do was dance, dance, dance.

In turning the boogeyman of twentieth-century Jewish life—the boogeyman of the twentieth century—into a shmuck, a show business shmuck, Brooks could also call on a genealogy outside of Hitler jokes. His old 2,000-Year-Old Man party host Moss Hart's writing partner, George S. Kaufman, had written a play in 1925 called *Butter and Egg Man*, the title referring—in arguably the most goyish way possible—to an out-of-town shmuck, a yahoo long on the folding stuff and short on intellect or taste. In Kaufman's original play, along with a number of its later filmed iterations, it turns out the unscrupulous producers are the shmucks; and the twists were pleasurable enough to support numerous adaptations, including a 1932 version starring the comedian Joe E. Brown and a 1953 musical version. In Brown's version, *The Tenderfoot*, the show is supposed to be a drama, but it's so badly done the audience thinks it's a comedy and it becomes an enormous hit.

Kaufman, one of the leading comic lights of his generation, had worked extensively with the Marx Brothers. If Groucho, Chico, and Harpo specialized in a kind of peekaboo ethnic disguise—about how these strange collections of misfits were pretending to be the kinds of misfits they weren't—then Kaufman frequently did them one better, creating characters with the aches and pains of American Jews, but not the mien or speech patterns. (Kaufman directed the original production of *The Front Page*, for example, and you can kind of imagine that rapid-fire patter in Yiddish-accented English.) But if the Butter and Egg Man, or, Who's the Shmuck?, had an appeal for Brooks, the goyishe precincts of 1920s Broadway had to go. In the postwar '60s, show business was out-and-out Jewish. So take the plot and talk about what it was really about—Jews hustling other people who won't get with the program, and then, in some sense, revealing themselves to be losers beyond the conceptions of their original loserdom. Or, to put it in a way that Brooks might love: it's like the story about the guy who's such a big shmuck, there was a shmuck contest and he came in second place. Why? Because he's such a shmuck, he can't win. That's how big a shmuck he is. And, in this Jewish-saturated world, what could the apotheosis of an ostensible flop be? Well, it had to be Hitler: as Brooks said forty-five years later: "I had to figure out what would be a surefire flop, and I brainstormed for days and days until I came up with Hitler. I thought, nobody's going to stand up and cheer for Hitler, especially not in New York with so many Jews."[79]

As of January 1966, the press was still reporting that Brooks was thinking of *Springtime* as a Broadway comedy (and musing about casting Paul Anka as the lead).[80] The title had been taken from the long-running stage show *Springtime for Henry* starring Edward Everett Horton, first pronounced off the cuff at a press conference for *All-American*, and that was still its name when it acquired an eminent producer: Sidney Glazier, who'd just won an Oscar for the documentary *The Eleanor Roosevelt Story*.[81] Glazier had asked Brooks to pitch him, tell him the story rather than read the screenplay, and when his coffee went straight up his nose halfway through because he was laughing so hard, he knew he needed to make the film. He put up half the money, and got no takers for the other half except an independent producer, Joseph E. Levine.[82] Filming was announced to be taking place in spring(time) in New York, which meant that Brooks, now writer-director, had a deadline.

He began to work intensely and in earnest on the project with his amanuensis Alfa-Betty Olsen from mid-1966 on; Brooks needed to work with someone else because as per his standard practice—as a *Times* profile of the period put it delicately—he "rarely put down words in the traditional sense."[83] He would be shpritzing, shotgunning, not writing and typing. Olsen took that role, while also contributing creatively to the mix—another in the line of Brooks's shaping partners.

The only exception to this work was a last hurrah-slash-possible comeback moment for Caesar, *The Sid Caesar, Imogene Coca, Carl Reiner, Howard Morris Special*, an hourlong show that aired in early April 1967.[84] It was mostly expanded and varied versions of a lot of the old bits, but the nostalgic impulse tended to win out over more sober critical judgments: "a viewer would like to think that the hour stood on its own eight contemporary feet," one critic wrote, and "any nagging doubts are hereby dismissed, if only for old times sake."[85] The Television Academy of Arts and Sciences apparently felt the same way, awarding the special two Emmys, resulting in the first Emmy and Writers' Guild Awards for Brooks and a reminder that as you got further away from the original, nostalgia played better and better.[86]

Still, Brooks was looking to the future. He wasn't at the Emmy Awards in June that same year; his focus was on his movie, filming in May through July of 1967 (after a scheduling change), which now had a new title: *The Producers*.[87] The revision spoke volumes. The most important element was featured front and center in the revised title: the most important thing wasn't the play itself, but the scheme, and the schemers. And the most important schemer was the man whose face Brooks had gotten planted with a custard pie a few years earlier.

Zero Mostel had weathered the tribulations of the blacklist to take the theater world by storm, first in off-Broadway venues (he originated the title role in *Rhinoceros*, Eugene Ionesco's "man exemplifies his bestial inhumanity" postmodern fable, snorting and groaning his way across the stage like a force of nature), then in *Forum*, and, most recently, in his triumphant turn in Jerry Bock and Sheldon Harnick's *Fiddler on the Roof*. Playing Tevye, the role of a lifetime, Mostel gave theatergoers a sense—among much else—of Jewish physicality in a way that no one had seen since Sid Caesar, and most of America didn't know Caesar was Jewish. There was the voice, of course, as Tevye exists originally, in Sholem Aleichem's series of short stories, as a voice, monologuing to the author-recorder, demanding, plaintively complaining, joking, deflecting, moralizing, psychologizing, theologizing, quoting, and much else. But Mostel—providing the constantly incongruous image of a heavy man dancing lightly on his feet, the concretization of the metaphor of the Jewish existence between earth and heaven, a portrait by Marc Chagall with theology by Abraham Heschel, provided a new template for viewers to see the Jewish body.

Fiddler on the Roof is, of course, an unspoken text behind *The Producers*, and not only because its star once played Tevye. Mostel complained after finishing his run in *Fiddler* that he was constantly being offered "Jewish family plays. If there's anything I hate it's family plays. *Mishpuche* plays, I call them," and you can practically hear the *khhhhh* coming off the pages of the *Los Angeles Times*.[88] But *The Producers*, in its own way, *is* about a Jewish family, and, of course, about a Jewish play, and about Jewish play as well. Mostel's character name, Bialystock, is not only reminiscent of the alt-bagel that you could pick up at Zabar's after a matinee, but is also a central Jewish city in Eastern Europe. (Brooks mentioned both these etymologies in interviews, also suggesting that "phonetically, it captures a big fat Jewish man.")[89] Bialystock the city, not coincidentally, had significant presence in Jewish America thanks to its *landsman* organizations—linking Mostel's character to the vanished shtetl almost as concretely as Bock and Harnick's Anatevka. *Fiddler* was a smash success in the mid-1960s, breaking the record for longest-running Broadway show at the time, and providing an "authentic" counterbalance to the development of American Jewish culture. If "Jewish comedy" was increasingly American-centric and satirical, *Fiddler* presented the other side of the coin: history-drenched and, because of that, ironic.

And Max Bialystock is a Tevye without the irony. It's Tevye, after all, who sings "If I Were a Rich Man"; and if the lesson he learns in *Fiddler* is that money isn't everything, then Max—who is the undiluted essence of wanting, shouting it out to Lincoln Center in a classic Mostel bellow—never learns his lesson at all. (Spoiler alert: the movie ends with him up to his old tricks in jail.) In that sense, Bialystock draws another card from the deck of Jewish folk archetypes: the *schnorrer*, who, in classic Jewish fashion, has his own chutzpah. The schnorrer—so much more than just a beggar—has a physical potency that eludes most of his ilk. In Freud's joke, the schnorrer goes to an expensive doctor in Vienna for a consultation, informs him he cannot pay the bill, and then, when asked why he signed up, shouts, "For my health, nothing is too expensive!" He will clearly live, like Bialystock, to a hundred and twenty. You can imagine him pounding his ostensibly weakened chest while he says it.

Max Bialystock is a man who makes his money by physically seducing little old ladies, and he seems to do it a lot. The character was inspired by a theatrical figure Brooks had worked for back in the 1940s, Benjamin Kutcher, who apparently used the same technique. "He made love to old ladies for money," Brooks said. "He lived out of the office. He ate a porridge—I don't know what it was—something between chicken soup, oatmeal, and barley. . . . He had one suit and one 'change,' which was a robe. When the suit was being cleaned, he couldn't go out." He is a creature of the physical; he sweats, he froths; he jumps and shouts and pops his eyes and rubs his hands and generally does anything he can for the money. "A living crescendo of flesh and noise," was how Brooks put it in an early sketch for the character.[90] And he torments Leo Bloom.

Brooks had met Gene Wilder when he'd worked with Bancroft in a Broadway production of Bertolt Brecht's *Mother Courage* in 1963; that summer, he invited him to Fire Island and read him the first three scenes of *Springtime for Hitler*.[91] If Mostel is the TNT of *The Producers*, then Gene Wilder, who plays Bloom, is the neutron bomb: quieter—generally—but absolutely deadly, and capable (as Brooks knows, and deploys to great effect in later collaborations) of remarkable rage. But it is a rage that gains its comic strength from sublimation, which is, as many have said, a prime characteristic of Jewish comedy as well. Bloom, James Joyce's Jew, he of the wandering and contemplating, has great depths to him. They are, of course, depths that are shot through with anxiety and neurosis, but you can't have everything.

Or can you? Because Bloom is it all: both child and man (remember that part of his baby blanket he has to carry around with him?), genius and idiot, winner and loser. If much of the character arc of *The Producers* is about Bialystock trying to convince Bloom to let his freak flag fly—one of the many allegories in Brooks's movies for Brooks-figures convincing others to accept his own ethos, he himself saying the name Bloom had "the right soft sound of a little weed opening into a flower"—then the other educational arc is Bloom convincing Bialystock that sometimes subtle sleight of hand is the best bet; an accounting trick will make more money than screwing little old ladies (in both senses of the word).[92] Some of this was replicated in the dynamic behind the scenes: the overpowering, experienced Mostel and the nervous neophyte Wilder—*The Producers* was only his second movie, after *Bonnie and Clyde*—although seeing Wilder's performance, Mostel stepped up his game.[93] And both of them, of course, are therefore Brooks, as he'd explicitly acknowledge a decade later; id and superego dancing about one another.[94]

Of course, the scheme within the movie doesn't work, despite being seemingly foolproof; and this falls into the category of "Jewish luck," of the "If I went into the hat business, people would be born without heads" variety. But it also fails precisely because of the broadness of the choice. If *Springtime for Hitler* had been subtly vile instead of across-the-board bad, it would have succeeded by failing . . . although then, of course, it wouldn't have been funny. The fact that it is in such horrendous taste is, of course, its saving-ruining grace. It even fails in failing, like the shmuck in that contest.

The question was always going to be how the audience would react—something Brooks was certainly aware would be an issue. Despite his long and recently increasingly successful résumé, he'd had great difficulties funding the project. Lew Wasserman, one of the most powerful figures in the business, did agree to take it on—on the condition that they change the play within the movie to a different Axis leader. Brooks, realizing *Springtime for Mussolini* wasn't going to land the same comic punch, demurred.[95] One reason the name was changed from *Springtime for Hitler* to *The Producers*, in fact, was that the producer Joseph E. Levine—who'd made his money on sword-and-sandal beefcake pictures like *Hercules*, then moved on to work on projects with David Susskind and distribute Fellini films in America—raised funds for Jewish charities and would be embarrassed by the title. Even the obstreperous Mostel almost didn't take the Bialystock role over a related "is it good for the Jews" issue. "What is this?" he shouted at Brooks. "A Jewish producer going to bed with old women on the brink of the grave? I can't play such a part. I'm a Jewish person." He relented only at his wife's urging.[96]

But it wasn't just Jewish sensibilities. There were a lot of people in America who were going to find the whole thing sort of . . . unseemly. Nazi kicklines? A writer—a crackpot, of course, but still—*praising* the Führer? When Brooks suggested the infamous overhead shot of the swastika kickline, the choreographer, Alan Johnson, said: "Oh my God . . . are we allowed to show this? Can we show this anywhere?"[97] Brooks would double down on his ethos of ridicule. "I got something like two hundred letters from rabbis and people of authority protesting *Springtime for Hitler*," he said. "'How dare you? This is shocking. People died in concentration camps and you're using Nazis for comedy.' I wrote back to each and every Jew who wrote to me and explained that you can't bring down despots, dictators, and murderers like Hitler by getting on the same soapbox with them. The only way to win is to humiliate them, to heap comedy on them and make them ridiculous. That's how you win."[98]

In this sense, the movie's most important scene—at least, the one most crucial to its self-definition as a comedy, and as a satire—takes place immediately after the big "Springtime for Hitler" number. The number comes to its finish—yes, with Nazi kickline—and Brooks cuts to the audience. Who are, every one of them, horrified by what they have just seen. (Well, all but one of them: a single man stands up and applauds the number, only to be set upon by the audience.) The patrons begin to leave: in droves, it looks like. Bialystock and Bloom, feeling their job is done, retire happily to the bar. But then the show starts in earnest—the laughable, ridiculous show, with its absurd, pathetic Hitler, its overblown overacting, its leaden rhetoric—and the audience notices. "It's funny!" someone shouts, teaching the rest of the audience—of *Springtime for Hitler,* and, of course, of *The Producers*—how to watch what they are seeing. And, so understanding, they lead to *Springtime*'s success, and thus its failure, and thus *The Producers*' success, setting a template—if a difficult criterion—for the biggest question in comedy: if it's funny, it's allowed. Or is it?

The production was embattled, with Mostel and Brooks both wielding their big personalities. One journalist visiting the set reported on this exchange: "'Zero,' Mel implored the too-antic actor the other morning, 'Be good. Carl Reiner is here and you're making me look terrible.' 'So blindfold him,' Zero suggested."[99] A *New York Times* profile of the filmmaker on set gave, underneath the genteel language of the arts profile, a picture of a catastrophe, a train wreck in the making. "I asked if he planned to do more directing. . . . 'I don't know. I don't know how these lying interviews go . . . what good does it do us now, this story? Save this and give it to me when the picture comes out. If the story came out in November it could be valuable to the film company. What good does it do us now?" The journalist reported on him "hurl[ing] vivid invective at one of his staff people, and sarcasm at a visiting photographer . . . a movie set is rarely the most serene of all possible worlds, but on this one tensions seemed tenser." A man came over to the journalist: "I'm Sidney Glazier. They call me the producer. Pray for me." (Brooks eventually banned Glazier from the set.)[100]

Glazier presumably was praying even harder after the brutal preview in Philadelphia—"it opened before an audience of 15 . . . with the outside temperature hovering around six below zero," which Brooks would later call, on many occasions, "the worst night of my life."[101] And, in some cases, the reviews matched. Not in all, certainly; in its first, brief appearance in theaters toward the end of 1967, the *Washington Post*'s critic said that he "roared like drains in April," comparing Bialystock and Bloom to "the glorious frauds of W.C. Fields and Groucho Marx."[102] The *Baltimore Sun*'s review called much of the film "hilarious"; the *Chicago Tribune* said Brooks was "incredibly impressive in his first feature attempt." *Variety* gave it a positive review, particularly praising the performances; and, in a gesture that gave the movie a tailwind, particularly among cognoscenti and industry audiences, Peter Sellers, Inspector Clouseau himself, saw an early print and took out full-page ads in trade papers praising its genius. "Last night I saw the ultimate film," was the first line. (It should also be noted that, according to the future American Jewish director Paul Mazursky, who was there, everyone in the Sellers screening was stoned.)[103] But even its fans had concerns, especially about Brooks's direction. The *Sun* pipped Brooks for letting "routines go on long after they have exhausted their comic potential." The *Christian Science Monitor* noted that Brooks's "screenplay is lively, but it fails to stand up under the onslaught of his direction . . . the sledgehammer approach employed to help [his material] off the screen has proved overly damaging." And Andrew Sarris, in the *Village Voice*, wrote that with the exception of a few sequences, "the direction of Mel Brooks is thoroughly vile and inept."[104]

And then there were the reactions to the larger conceptual impact of the work. That *Sun* review had opened by explicitly linking *The Producers* to *Bonnie and Clyde*, the film frequently considered ground zero of the New Hollywood move away from studio-centered production, and the embrace of the individual voices of filmmakers who reflected the concerns of the counterculture. "Not long ago in a review of the film *Bonnie and Clyde*," the reviewer wrote, "I indicated—somewhat facetiously—that it wouldn't surprise me if someday somebody came up with a sympathetic treatment of the story of Eva Braun and Adolph Hitler. Well, they have." Renata Adler, in her review for the *Times*, called it "a violently mixed bag. Some of it is shoddy and gross and cruel; the rest is funny in an entirely unexpected way." She summed up the perspective of the general culturati by throwing up her hands and asking: What's next—a movie making light of Hiroshima? Of cancer? Of "malformity"?[105] Arthur Schlesinger, Jr., reviewing the movie for *Vogue* (!), opened: "The question before the house is: When can bad taste lead to good movies?" His answer was: certainly not in this case. "It seemed to me to be an almost flawless triumph of bad taste, unredeemed by charm or style. . . . *The Producers* is warmly recommended for all those who regard the following things as hilarious: Hitler, Nazis, queers, hysterics, old ladies being pawed, and infantilism."[106] But perhaps the most insightful comment came from Pauline Kael.

Kael was in the process of establishing her iconic role as a champion of the New Hollywood. She also spoke as the leader of a new generation of critics for whom cinema had always been the predominant cultural medium, who fluently spoke (and appreciated) the language of cinema and reserved her greatest praise for those who did the same. Which is another way of saying that she was less interested in those who approached cinema as more of a newer medium or a non-native one: for example, Brooks, whose outsider's eye always allowed him to flourish on the aesthetic margins, but not—at least in Kael's view—come to the center of the discourse. It felt old-fashioned.

Her review of *The Producers*, accordingly, marked it as "unconventional" because it was "so amateurishly crude, and because it revels in the kind of show-business Jewish humor that used to be too specialized for movies."[107] Claiming *The Producers* as a specifically Jewish movie, and a specifically Jewish comedy, presented it as a kind of fellow traveler in New Hollywood movies featuring non-Aryan leading figures like Elliott Gould, Richard Dreyfuss, and—perhaps more relevantly for Brooks—Dustin Hoffman, starring with his wife in *The Graduate*, which appeared in theaters a month after *The Producers* first opened. (Had he not been cast in *The Graduate*, he would have appeared in *The Producers*—in the role of Liebkind, *Springtime for Hitler*'s author, eventually played with masterful madness by Kenneth Mars.)[108] It would also end up being the case for Gene Wilder, who pursued his own odd form of movie stardom through the 1970s and early '80s. Kael's marginalization of Brooks's form of Jewish comedy as lesser film comedy, though, helped contribute to the through-line that centered Woody Allen as the leading figure in Jewish film comedy in the '70s, the comedian's version of Gould and Hoffman and Dreyfuss, rather than Brooks—who, as we'll see, would become massively more commercially successful.

But to go back and focus on that "amateurishly crude": focusing on Kael's and Adler's examination of crudity and cruelty would neglect another way of reading *The Producers*. The *Tribune*'s reviewer had actually linked the crudity to the question of offensiveness, marking it, insightfully, as a creative choice:

"treating his potentially-tastefully [*sic*] Nazi nonsense with strictly in-bounds broad burlesque." But it falls to their fellow critic Susan Sontag to articulate the meaning of the movie in another way: as a significant development of Brooks's camp aesthetic. *The Producers* was composed, produced, and released during the high point of camp as idea. ("The visit to the transvestite director degenerates into a tiresome anthology of camp mannerisms," one review read.)[109] Sontag's essay "Notes on Camp," which first appeared in *Partisan Review* in 1964, received even broader circulation when it was published in her first book of essays, *Against Interpretation*, in 1966; and the concept had become entrenched in popular culture that same year, thanks to television. Any American with a TV set in 1966, and certainly someone in the industry like Brooks, was unquestionably aware of the Bat-mania sweeping the country thanks to the massive success of the *Batman* television show. It dominated the airwaves during the second season of *Get Smart*, and it was constantly identified by critics and consumers as a camp program. (The network had invited Andy Warhol to the premiere.)

In that same theater scene discussed earlier, a rich-looking female theatergoer, watching the "Springtime for Hitler" number, claps her hand to her mouth and shouts, "Well! Talk about bad taste!" Talk about it, indeed. Brooks revels in it; whether camp is about excess, shock, or knowing artifice (and what is a movie about the behind-the-scenes production of a show, calling attention to the men behind the curtain as literally the main focus, other than artifice), *The Producers* had it. And, as Mostel puts it, if you've got it, you flaunt it. Jews are hardly the sole or the main expositors of camp: for many decades, camp has been identified as a hallmark of gay aesthetics, and it's not surprising that characters who share all the signs of coded and not-so-coded gay identity also appear in *The Producers*. (The *Tribune*'s reviewer, in language reminding us that times have thankfully changed, described one character as "fruity as a slot machine" and another as "a swishy Svengali.") You don't need to go into stereotypes about the prevalence of gays and Jews in the theater to read Brooks as commenting on both.

Ultimately, though, Brooks's particular brand of envelope-pushing didn't mesh with the times' call for change, for a sense of the New: that was sewn up by his partners, through a strange set of logistical circumstances. *The Producers* was almost inextricably connected with *The Graduate*, which was executive produced by Brooks's producer Joseph E. Levine, its screenplay co-written by *Get Smart* co-creator Buck Henry, directed by former TV special colleague Mike Nichols, and of course starring wife Anne Bancroft. But in terms of celebration and commerce, there was no contest.

The Graduate became one of the highest-grossing movies of the decade, and as of 2020, adjusted for inflation, in the top 25 of all time; *The Producers* made, at best, two percent of its domestic box office.[110] The balance was a little less lopsided when it came to the Academy Awards, but not much. Even though *The Producers* appeared on screen only a month before *The Graduate*, the Academy's rules for eligibility—namely, when a film premieres in Los Angeles County—meant that they competed in separate years for the Oscar awards. *The Graduate*—Nichols's simmering tale of rebellious anomie drenched in irony and California sunshine—picked up seven nominations, including for Nichols, Hoffman, Bancroft, Henry (with partner Calder Willingham), along with best picture, best supporting actress for Katharine Ross, and best cinematography; it won only the best director prize. As for *The Producers*, Wilder, in a performance so ferocious that it was impossible to ignore, received a nomination for best supporting actor, in a category largely though not entirely dominated by studio pictures, with actors from *Oliver!*, *Star!*, and *The Subject Was Roses* also nominated (the one New Hollywood figure, Seymour Cassel from the John Cassavetes film *Faces*, also didn't win). But more important, Brooks walked away with the trophy for best original screenplay, in a category that demonstrated the changing balance between the Old and New: the other nominees were Cassavetes for *Faces*, Stanley Kubrick for *2001*, Ira Wallach and Peter Ustinov for *Hot Millions*, and Franco Solinas and Gillo Pontecorvo for *The Battle of Algiers*.

"I want to thank the Academy of Arts, Sciences, and Money," Brooks said upon receiving the award.[111] An insider's joke; and it's certainly not impossible, looking at the field, to argue that Brooks was the conservative insider candidate here, and it's certainly the case—ultimately—that the movie is, at its social and cultural heart, a conservative one. Yes, it breaks new ground in representing bad taste; bringing camp to the big screen; making manifest the subtext of Jewishy showbiz. But ultimately, it's another entry in the show-about-a-show genre, which has whiskers on its whiskers; its beats are taken from Old Broadway; its satirical barbs of the flower child Lorenzo St. Dubois, or LSD for short, are weak and, let's be honest, kind of square; and its set pieces are reminiscent—as parodies are—of moments from all sorts of earlier movies and productions.[112] Which again is not surprising, given the title and the aim: producers package, after all. They put things together. Sometimes in new and surprising ways, always aiming for them to be attention-getting, but the producers' job is to get and hold an audience. And that was what Brooks had been trying to do since that first patter song of his, and what he would continue to do for the next decades.

With one surprising, and seemingly uncharacteristic, swerve.

Although you could hardly characterize *The Producers* as an unqualified success, at least from an industry perspective, if it *was* a failure—and isn't that the Jewish way, success in failing—it was, in the manner of Hollywood (at least toward white men), a success that allowed Brooks to fail upward, and get financing for a follow-up movie. But even the notoriously unpredictable Brooks made a remarkably unpredictable choice: to adapt a novel by two Russian-Jewish writers, Ilya Ilf and Yevgeni Petrov, for the screen. Their novel from 1928, *The Twelve Chairs*, is a knockabout picaresque: in the failing days of the *ancien régime*, aristocrats have sewed their fortune in jewels into one of the twelve chairs that adorned their dining room. Those chairs, on the dissolution of the household (and the family), are scattered to the four winds: relatives, priests, and con artists who have been let in on the secret scramble to recover them and keep the fortune for themselves.

Brooks claimed the work had been an idée fixe of his since the 1950s. He has claimed he had come across the story first as a teenager in the library, which is possible—it had come out in 1930 under the title *Diamonds to Sit On*—and that he had received the book from Mel Tolkin—not implausible, given Tolkin's role in introducing him to Russian literature.[113] But probably most plausible is that Brooks's formative encounter with the story would have been in the very loose film adaptation that appeared in 1945, with its own Jewish genealogy: a teen-aged Brooks would have undoubtedly have watched *It's In the Bag!* if for no other reason than it starred his great comic hero Jack Benny. Benny's *To Be or Not to Be* later turned out to be the only other remake Brooks did, as we'll see; and if Benny hadn't been enough to make an impression, the movie also starred Fred Allen and featured a cavalcade of present and future stars ranging from Don Ameche to Robert Benchley to William Bendix, most of whom play themselves. (In that version, Allen plays—I'm not making this up—the ringmaster of a flea circus whose inheritance is hidden in some of the chairs.)

The Twelve Chairs is surely Brooks's least-known film, and, in many ways, seems the least on-brand for a Brooks film. He explained his choice to make the movie, in part, by saying, "I'm a Russian Jew, and finally, I could bathe in everything Russian that's in me . . . it would be like if a fourth-generation American black visited Africa and felt the country on his skin and in his bones. He wouldn't want to live there, but maybe, he'd want to swim in that river just once."[114] But the particular type of Russian Jewishness on display in *The Twelve Chairs*—or, more precisely, Russian Jewishness refracted through a very American Jewish sensibility—might be best expressed by comparing it with another comedy about the Russian literary landscape produced by an American Jewish comedian five years later: Woody Allen's 1975 film *Love and Death*.

Allen's approach, while suffused with the rhythms and touchstones of Russian literary and cinematic life, is, uncharacteristically, the far more parodic of the two films: think, for example, of the moment in which he and Diane Keaton look off into space and speak of wheat. It also derives much of its parody from the Judaization of the grand narratives of Russian literature: the inherent joke of the movie is the possibility (or impossibility) of the nebbish to move through this deeply Gentile (and often forbiddingly Christian, or forbiddingly physical and masculine) Slavic space. Conversely, *The Twelve Chairs*—a rarity for Brooks—plays its comedy straight.

The lead, Frank Langella—well known to Brooks from having starred with Bancroft in *A Cry of Players* at Lincoln Center as the young William Shakespeare—was not only another figure from the theater, but a "Potential Matinee Idol," according to the *Times* in his very first interview: in it, Langella called Brooks "one of the few men in the world I would trust with my life."[115] Gentile, perhaps not needless to say; he would become a sex symbol playing Dracula both on Broadway and in the movies. The Jewish subtext that Ilf and Petrov's writing makes clear in the original—which is, in some way, about the question of the possibility of Jewish prospects scrambling for survival in the ever-changing Soviet Union—largely vanishes in the comedy, led by Langella and Dom DeLuise. (Langella and Bancroft used to whisper "little Italian things . . . to each other on stage if anything goes wrong.")

Perhaps it doesn't vanish entirely: the catchy song Brooks co-wrote with John Morris, with a strong assist from Brahms, playing over the title credits, "Hope for the best/expect the worst," may be the most Brooksian thing about the movie, and his description of Langella's character as "a rogue, a man who lives not by decree, but by his wits," is a useful description not just of Brooks thinking about himself, but about the Jewish way of surviving under persecution. Brooks also described the movie in a manner faithful to its novelistic origins as "about two guys who can't live under Communism," and although the creator of *Get Smart* was as perfectly capable of channeling a general Cold War anti-Communist ethos as anyone else, there's probably something more particularly, Jewishly, personal to it for him, too.[116] Brooks once said in an interview, explaining the roots of his comedy, that "When the tall, blond Teutons have been nipping at your heels for thousands of years, you find it enervating to keep wailing. So you make jokes. If your enemy is laughing, how can he bludgeon you to death?"[117]

In that sense, *The Twelve Chairs*, while being—at best—about Jews in very good and not-so-good disguise, is about another staple of Jewish comedy: the role of wit to get out of the most impossible situations. In specific historical and narrative context, certainly, but also more generally, as a historical ethos. It's also about, without spoiling the end of the movie, how ultimately everything *but* surviving via wit falls away, because other solutions are revealed to be, in the end, fantasies. Both *The Producers* and *The Twelve Chairs*, in their own ways, are about the success of failure and the privileging of the journey over journey's end: which is, in its own way, the crux of diaspora Jewish history, which is all about the genius of living through—and thriving in, and making art of—an eternal middle. If the messianic era ever comes, that's the end of the show.

The wink here—the intrusion of the Jew—is of course Brooks himself. Despite his increasing confidence as a performer, he hadn't appeared at all in *The Producers*. But his role in *The Twelve Chairs*—a scene-stealer of a part, where, not coincidentally, he can stand off to the side and tummel, attracting attention (and good notices, by Kael, no less, among many others), commenting on the action without being part of it, being disguised while letting the disguise show, is Brooks at his essence.[118] Of course, he had a good line about the process, papering over ambitions and intents and turning himself—in two senses— into a joke: "I ran out of money, and I was the cheapest actor I could find."[119] The disguise, by its nature, is an incongruity, the beginning of Brooks appearing in movies in roles that at times replicate Jewish jokes and rumors about the strange vicissitudes of Jews moving through history; a wink to the idea—a conspiracy theory exploded through laughter and ridicule—that Jews can show up *anywhere*. This will return in later works.

Perhaps Brooks, stung by the criticism of his work as too vaudeville, too crude, too broad, too Jewishy showbiz, wanted to go the other way entirely. To get *respect*. "I don't want to be considered a stuffy, preposterous intellectual," he said in an interview at the time of *The Twelve Chairs*' release. "But I am one of the brightest people you're gonna run into in your life. . . . I'm a very serious comedy writer, just as Nikolai Gogol, Isaac Babel, [Sean] O'Casey, Jonathan Swift, Henry Fielding were. I mean, I don't think I'm exactly small fry."[120] He couldn't do it by taking on the mantle of the counterculture: he'd already been marginalized, and it wasn't a good fit anyway. He couldn't take the path of his contemporary Martin Scorsese, delving into his background of gritty urbanism and conflicted faith—Brooks's Jewishness was never particularly religious. So he turned to the closest thing he could find, that cultural patrimony from Big Mel and the work they did together on *Your Show of Shows*: the foreign film, but something more than that this time. Something closer to the real thing: after all, it's still a comedy if you adapt a comic novel.

In that respect, it's worth noting that Brooks's substantive encounter with Eastern European literature predates not only Allen's, but another American Jewish comedian's serious turn in that arena. In the year between *The Producers* and *The Twelve Chairs*, another Jewish comic phenomenon came out that took Brooks's record for bad taste and left it shattered in the dust: or, perhaps more precisely, wrapped up in a violated piece of liver. Philip Roth's *Portnoy's Complaint* was *also* deeply crude (although no one could accuse the bravura novel of being "amateurish" in any way), extremely Jewish, vulgar, and even, in its own way, very showbizzy. Portnoy, and *Portnoy*, is constantly referring to popular culture, name-checking Henny Youngman and referring to American popular film as the touchstone of acculturation; his final mental breakdown/breakthrough is couched in terms taken directly from the iconic 1949 gangster film *White Heat*—one of the few powerful genres of American film, intriguingly, that Brooks never dedicated a full-fledged parody to.

As *Portnoy* came out, Roth demonstrated his intellectual bona fides in a clever response he gave to the inevitable questions about literary and comedic influences. Asked if he was influenced by the funny "sick" stand-up comedians of the day, he gave an answer that put him in similar channels to Brooks, a conservative answer hearkening back to earlier days: he said he was influenced by a very funny sit-down comic named Franz Kafka. Roth would go on to explore this Eastern European connection further: his post-*Portnoy* work—editing the Voices from the Other Europe series and using his prestige to introduce a raft of Eastern European writers to American audiences, not least the grand metaphysical comedian Milan Kundera—could be seen, in some ways, as a trajectory following in Brooks's footsteps, or at least the two walking in partnership. Brooks himself made a Kafka joke in *The Producers*, when Bialystock rejects "The Metamorphosis" as the basis of his Broadway flop in "quizzical disgust."[121] Because of the siloing of American culture and, in some ways, the sidelining of Brooks based on his past and context, that of course didn't happen. But wouldn't it have been funny if it had?

Brooks filmed *The Twelve Chairs* behind the Iron Curtain, in Yugoslavia in 1969, where the authoritarian ruler of the country, Josip Broz Tito, could get anything a film production needed. Extras in Hollywood then could earn $75 a day; in Yugoslavia, "the going price . . . is $4 a day," Brooks said. "They not only bring their own lunch, they'll bring you some. The only hardship was wood. Eating wood three times a day."[122] The movie was released in October 1970 to lukewarm reviews and not great business (although apparently Princess Margaret ordered a private screening of the film, if the columnists can be believed).[123] "I wouldn't be surprised if Brooks had seen the tale as a fairly thoughtful parable," summed up the *Los Angeles Times*, "but what has survived is a plot and an insufficiency of jokes." Before production, Brooks had fumed: "I'll show these cockamamie *Cahiers* critics. I'll make a movie that'll bend their bagels."[124] But the bagels, alas, remained resolutely unbent.

As a result, Brooks was even less desirable around the film industry than before, and was looking for projects that already had something of a track record, or, at least, some heat around them. And maybe something that was more up his alley: that is to say, edgy, but not intellectual. It wasn't "Have You Heard, Bronsky Is Dying?" a potential Mostel vehicle about a garment industry titan who wanted to build himself a pyramid in the suburbs. It wasn't an adaptation of Oliver Goldsmith's *She Stoops to Conquer*, although that got as far as an announcement; or a weak *Get Smart*-esque retread called "Inspector Benjamino"; or even a syndicated Reiner-hosted program called *The Comedians*, which featured lots of funny folks shooting the shit on a theme.[125] It *certainly* wasn't doing warmed-over Ballantine Brewmaster shtick for a new felt-tip pen called the Bic Banana, even if it did help Bic "capture 20 percent of the market in porous-point pens."[126]

Brooks had known, at least inchoately, what he was grop-
ing toward. As he would later say: "If you were a Jewish intellectual, whose parents had emigrated from Russia, you could like
my pictures, but there were hardly any of those in Amarillo,
Texas, where you gotta play in one of their three or four theaters or else you're outa luck. You gotta get into one of the John
Wayne houses or you ain't ever gonna break out."[127] He'd know
it when he saw it: how to get into those John Wayne houses.
And then the screenplay landed on his desk, and he saw it.

About a black sheriff named Tex X.

3

Breaking Clichés

Brooks had grown up in the golden age of the Western, watching those wide open landscapes and those tough-talking men stride their way across the screen. On *Your Show of Shows,* he and others had parodied the Westerns of the 1950s—most notably *Shane,* featuring the man who strides in, and out, of town, totally alone. ("Come back, Shane!" moviegoers—and parodists—of a certain age can hear. "Come back!") As a television producer, Brooks understood the power of the Western mythos: with shows like *Gunsmoke* and *Bonanza* seemingly slated to never go off the air, it was a versatile idea that seemed to work in any medium.

In some ways, this sense of the Western as a myth calling for its own deconstruction had been made more pronounced by the surge in European interest in the genre that, thanks to the Italian filmmaker Sergio Leone, became generally known, at first pejoratively, as the "spaghetti western." In postwar

Europe, inundated by American mass culture in the wake of re-building sponsored by the Marshall Plan, American imagination became the wall European artists bounced their creative impe-tus off. *A Fistful of Dollars*, directed by Leone and starring Clint Eastwood, came out in 1964, around the same time Brooks was taking on the icon of Cold War masculinity known as the super-spy, and came to America three years later, bringing new ap-proaches and perspectives to the genre along with it. It may not be surprising that the leading trope of the spaghetti western—mysterious stranger comes into town where people are fight-ing, takes control of things, and cleans it up/plays boss—can in some sense be seen as a central metaphor for American postwar intervention and its generally positive but also warily concern-ing aspect. Right is on their side, but at what cost? And what does it say about the character?

For Brooks, the Western myth similarly yielded questions of morality and rectitude: but, ever the outsider, he thought of them not by who was anchoring the picture but by who wasn't in it. For him, that was Jews. (As we already saw, on *Your Show of Shows* the secret tell of Shane was that he ate herring.) But for America as a whole, there were others who were absent. It's in this sense we might think of *Blazing Saddles*—which was first announced to the public under the title *Black Bart*—as a *Guess Who's Coming to the Campfire Dinner?* The earlier film, released the year before *The Producers* (and, not incidentally, winning the Oscar in the same category Brooks did, best original screen-play, that previous year), is also a version of the spaghetti west-ern, but conceived in the crucible of the civil rights movement: someone unexpected walks into an all-white space and discom-fort ensues. But instead of using the framework to preach an object lesson in a creaky melodrama, Brooks plays the chaos for comedy: in many ways giving a much more insightful view of a certain kind of racism endemic to the American imagination about itself, and showing characters who, even on the side of the angels, are more complicated than the plaster saint played by Sidney Poitier, or even the fragile (in all senses) liberalism of Spencer Tracy and Katharine Hepburn.

This focus on something other than Jewishness as the outsider lens came in no small part from the fact that the project didn't originate with Brooks. The first draft of the screenplay—then titled *Tex X*—was by Andrew Bergman, who'd written a doctorate on films of the Depression before turning his hand to fiction writing. *Tex X* had started life as a novella, but became a screenplay while Bergman worked as a film publicist for United Artists. As material in Hollywood does, it attracted heat—Alan Arkin was going to direct, James Earl Jones was going to play the sheriff—then fell apart; and so the script was available.

Brooks was told about it by his agent David Begelman (soon to become head of film production at Columbia Pictures). As Brooks retells the conversation, he didn't want to do it, but Begelman told him he had to: "Because you owe a fortune in alimony, because you are in debt, and because you have no choice."[1] Brooks didn't disagree. He picked it up and hired a team of writers for rewrites. "Write from the gut," he told them. "Write from the heart. Write the craziest shit." Now, unlike in the *Your Show of Shows'* writers room, *he* was the king. Everyone was pitching to *him*. *He* got to decide what was in and what was out. And like Caesar, he wasn't afraid of talent, or of yelling; and in Richard Pryor, he got both.

Brooks had felt they needed a Black voice in the room along with himself and the three other Jewish writers. He'd tried for Dick Gregory, who said no; then Norman Steinberg, who knew Pryor from the Flip Wilson show, suggested the prodigiously gifted and notoriously volatile comic. (Pryor offered cocaine to the four Jewish writers the first day. "Never before lunch," Brooks responded.)[2] Although Pryor left after the first revised draft, his imprint was unquestionably on the final product. One can imagine the road not taken if Warner Brothers,

which eventually took on the film, had not refused to approve
Pryor for the lead. (In protest, Brooks quit the picture for three
days.)[3] Pryor's volcanic talent, his ability to create comedy based
on simmering and seething anger, would have taken the movie
in a very different direction—less toward parody and more toward, perhaps, contemporary satire and allegory. The eventual
title change from *Black Bart* to *Blazing Saddles* was because the
studio "thought 'Black Bart' would be confused with the black-
action pictures being produced these days, and that people
wouldn't understand that it was a Western," according to Brooks,
who didn't seem particularly displeased with the change.[4] There
was something new in the air, something volatile and angry and
radical, in the Blaxploitation pictures of the era. This would be
subversive, and even revolutionary, but not like that.

The shift to a more conservative, more Brooksian approach
was effectuated by casting the Juilliard-trained and Tony-win-
ning television star Cleavon Little. Little took, under Brooks's
direction, a much more laid-back, *I Spy*–like approach to the
material, which allowed the other characters to overact in Brooks's
rule number one of ridicule: let the shmucks show themselves.
Take, for example, Bart's opening ride into town, where he greets
an elderly woman sweetly with a typical "Morning, ma'am.
And isn't it a lovely morning?" The reply: "Up yours," with an
N-word thrown in to boot. The audience would have held their
breath waiting for Pryor to jump off his horse and pound the
wrinkled little racist into powder. With Little, detached and
sardonic bemusement—wry disappointment, but not surprise—
is his way. It's both cool and, in its own way, more congruent
with a Jewish response to such displays. *Of course that's how it is,*
Little's look—and Brooks's direction—say. *Who would have expected Goytown, Population Whitebread to be any different? Not us.
We're not shmucks.* Or, as the movie pungently puts it: "You
gotta remember that these are just simple farmers . . . These

are people of the *land*. The common clay of the New West. . . . You know—*morons*."

Of course, their leader—the leading shmuck in the film—is played by Brooks. Once more making himself the butt of the joke so no one else can, the director presents himself as "the silver-tongued moron who's the governor of the territory."[5] Adopting an odd, herky-jerky style that reminded one British reviewer of "all the Jewish comedians one has ever seen who work noticeably hard for their effects," he presents himself as the clueless man in charge, catalyzing some of the chaos around him but by no means in control—a remarkable difference from the paternal image of Caesar.[6] Nobody here but us loons and idiots, goes the message. His character, Governor Le Pétomane, was not just a repeat habitual user of the N-word, though; he symbolizes another ethos of the production, too, his name taken as it was from a "celebrated French flatulist, whose Moulin Rouge act consisted of farting out cannon fire, musical notes, and animal noises (*pétomane* translates roughly as 'fartomaniac')."[7] Brooks's choice for the movie's new title, *Blazing Saddles*, was yet another reference to flatulence, maybe part of the reason he was all right with it; and the movie's most infamous scene, the roaring (sorry) return of Brooks as a poète maudit of bad taste, comes when a bunch of cowboys are eating baked beans and passing gas around a fire.

Brooks defended and explained the scene variously in interviews over the years. "As long as I am on the soapbox, farts will be heard!" he would say. Part of this, of course, a large part, was the same sense of parody that had served him well since the Caesar days. "Basically," he said, "it's me taking a look at the West based on all the cowboy movies I've seen in my life. Maybe 6,000."[8] An ad for the movie suggested that one should "Never give a saga an even break," and well before the movie was filming he was using that line about including every Western cliché in the hope of killing them off in the process.[9] And the camp-fire bean-eating scene, a cliché if there ever was one, led natu-rally, in Brooks's fertile and febrile imagination, to what came naturally: "I mean, you can't eat so many beans without some noise happening there." And the fact, for Brooks, that this had never appeared on screen—had never been *allowed* to appear—stood in, in its ridiculous way, for the sometimes unconsidered, often tepidly pusillanimous nature of the Hollywood establish-ment. "For 75 years, these big hairy brutes have been smashing their fists into each other's faces and blasting each other full of holes with six-guns, but in all that time, not one has had the courage to produce a fart. I think that's funny."[10]

And also perhaps dangerous, in its own way: a danger to the system no less pronounced—possibly more—than a Nazi kickline, which was so much more obviously out of bounds that it was easily marginalized. And *Blazing Saddles* turned out to be more dangerous than *that*, as its solution to an inherent struc-tural problem—how do you end the thing?—produced a deeper, more subversive point: not just pointing out the gaps and holes in the Western myth as it had been transmitted to film and television, racism foremost among them, but giving the sense it was all artifice, from top to bottom. Which explains the movie's ending, puzzling to some, in which the entire thing is revealed to be a Hollywood movie shooting on a backlot, as the big final fight crashes through and engulfs another movie being made, a big, splashy Busby Berkeley–type musical with dozens of male dancers in tuxedoes and top hats. It may not be coincidence that the first screening for Warner's studio executives went cat-astrophically, while the same cut run that night for non-exec studio employees—not stakeholders in the system—was a huge success.[11]

"Piss on you, I'm workin' for Mel Brooks!" says one griz-zled cowboy as he punches yet another of Brooks's fey directors in the stomach (after the man begs him: "Please! Not in the face!"). The scene redoubles the violation of the parodic tension between fidelity and exaggeration he's tried to establish through the movie in almost every previous moment. But for Brooks it was crucial, an artistic step forward. As he put it: "What I did when the gunfight spilled over onto the Busby Berkeley set with the fifty dancers was what Picasso did when he painted two eyes on the same side of the head." And all the writers, despite much discussion about who originated what with regard to other aspects of the film, agree this ending was Brooks's idea.[12]

What Brooks and *Blazing Saddles* do here, in an awful Western-flavored pun I apologize for herewith, is to strike camp; to deflate Western and, not coincidentally, Gentile notions of masculinity by juxtaposing them with the most over-exaggerated, hyper-effeminate, unmanly sensibility possible—certainly according to the norms of the time. The dancers are rehearsing a musical number called "The French Mistake," which, with its title—the term refers to a heterosexual man having a gay encounter he later regrets—and, well, suggestive lyrics and motions ("Throw out your hands, stick out your tush, hands on your hips, give them a push, you'll be surprised—you're doing the French mistake"), winkingly suggests the foundations of the whole system are built on sand. In one brief moment, a cowboy punches a dancer off-camera through a doorway; they return through another doorway immediately, and the cowboy, arm around the dancer, tells him, "I'm parked over near the commissary."

But the scene is also simultaneously a key to Brooks's structural foundations in his filmmaking. Brooks mused in an interview in 1977 that every one of his movies from *The Producers* to *Silent Movie* was also about "the love story between two men . . . which seems to be one of my motifs. Maybe my heaviest. I mean, I do love the fellowship of men . . . I don't know. Maybe I'm really a fag. But, seriously, I do love men; and I do love my men friends."[13] Bancroft, in an interview the next year, made the same point, saying: "Mel really loves men, he has a terrific sense of male camaraderie . . . His attitude towards women can be really primitive. When we have big rows, he yells, 'No more monogamy for me! Next time it'll be with a man!' He actually threatens me with Dom DeLuise!"[14] Brooks himself, around the same time, suggested that this longing for male companionship and comfort "goes back a lot further than sex. All the way to my father, whom I never really knew and can't remember."[15] The varying weights of homoerotic or homosocial fascination and autobiographical longing are certainly debatable, but both are undoubtedly present throughout Brooks's oeuvre.

This sense of performance, of code and disguise, of relationships obscured and blazing forth, is connected once more to a third striking moment of conscious artifice in *Blazing Saddles*. Unsurprisingly, it's another scene in which Brooks appears; this time playing a Yiddish-speaking Native American. "Shvartzes!" he exclaims, seeing a young Sheriff Bart with his parents. He then waves off a young brave brandishing a tomahawk: "Na, na, *zayt nisht meshuge* [Don't be crazy.]" Letting them go in Yinglish—"*khap* a walk!"—he then adds, in a mixture of Yiddish and English, "Have you ever seen anything like it in your life? They darker than us!" punctuating his line with a brief whoop.

The scene works on a dazzling variety of levels, a few of which are worth unpacking. The first, of course, plays with a historical legend—one perhaps particularly intriguing in the post-1967 days of Jewish triumphal historicism—that Native Americans were related to, or indeed were, the Ten Lost Tribes. Put aside the obvious point that even *were* they Jewish descendants they wouldn't be speaking Yiddish: they were Americans all along, was the point. They were there first. In this sense, also, Brooks suggests a kind of racial solidarity, in an era of attempts at Black-Jewish liberal partnership, with his line suggesting both community of and hierarchy among the oppressed.

(Is it just coincidence, or costumer's initiative, or directorial symbolic intent, that Brooks's war paint is red, white, and blue?)

That suggestion, of course, is spoken in a mixture of Yiddish and English, meaning that half of what Brooks is saying in the scene—though not the line "they darker than us"—is incomprehensible to most people watching *Blazing Saddles*, in precisely the same way that Native American speech in Westerns remains so to most observers. Or not precisely: because in many cases in classic Hollywood, "Native American speech" was just gibberish, composed as an act of artificiality by studios uninterested in hearing enough of the story to hear the story. (Which was brought home when John Wayne actually hired someone to provide "authentic" speech, and another private joke was born, there at Wayne's expense.)

Because in speaking Yiddish, Brooks was also playing, with cognoscenti and movie fans with long memories, on the fact that Jews had been playing Native Americans on stage and screen all the time. One of the most famous was Brooks's early employer and contact Eddie Cantor, who did it in the movie *Whoopee*, but Sophie Tucker did it, too, and his wife's most famous co-star, Dustin Hoffman, was doing it at that very moment, albeit in a dramatic key, in the film *Little Big Man*. In other words, to look at a Native American and see a Jew was not, or at least not only, an act of shared metaphorical alienation, or, for that matter, a case of cultural appropriation. That wasn't even primarily it, certainly not at the time. What you were looking at was *a show business professional.*[16]

Which is to say that by 1973, after all, the Western was *already* being deconstructed in the States by filmmakers like Robert Altman and Warren Beatty; and that Brooks, who gets—and deserves—a lot of credit for thinking that the traditional Western left something to be desired, something absent, is parodying the counter-Western as much as he is the ones by Howard Hawks and John Ford; the New Hollywood, which was never that congenial to his efforts, as well as the Old. If the stars of the revisionist Western still have a sober tragedy about them—as victims, martyrs, or monsters—Brooks is interested in saying *his* stars have nothing to do with it. Cleavon Little is a man out of time. Gene Wilder, an eleventh-hour replacement when the original actor Gig Young suffered an alcoholic relapse, is an oddly undramatic figure with hidden depths of action.[17] They are, instead, talented participants in revue, in this remarkable entry in the inside baseball business of show.

Which was, in some sense, the crux of the objectors' point. What we haven't talked about yet, weighed down by the meanings and depths of the movie, are the gags, which come fast and furious: Gucci saddlebags, desert tollbooths, Klan sheets with "Have a nice day" on them, everyone in town named Johnson. "*Spoof* is such a tiny word to describe this picture," Brooks said in a pre-release interview. "Even *zany*. I mean, it's *majestic* insanity."[18] Brooks always remembered going to the studio chief, John Calley, about some of the movie's excesses, asking if he could really do it; Calley's reply—"Mel, if you're going to go up to the bell, ring it," lingered long in Brooks's memory.[19] And ring it he did, so loudly that at times it threatened to drown everything else out. One review suggested that "Looking for messages in *Blazing Saddles* is like going to a weighing machine for advice. What Brooks wants us to do is to laugh our untroubled heads off, and he will try anything to achieve this welcome result."[20] A perspicacious British critic suggested, evoking Brooks's professional origins, that "his satirical talent still seems more appropriate to the undisguised fragmentation of the revue format than to the cumulative structures of even a skeleton narrative development . . . one suspects that the film's gradual disintegration derives not—as has been suggested—from its makers' inability to end it so much as from their inability to stop laughing at their own jokes."[21]

A parallel case in point was Brooks's effort to pave the way and raise his profile before the movie by releasing not only a collection of the three earlier 2,000-Year-Old Man records—as a 1973 "Christmas package," as the *Times* put it somewhat inappositely—but also another album, recorded in front of two hundred friends dining on cracked crab and chili from Chasen's restaurant on couches set up at a recording studio in Burbank.[22] Although the album received generally positive reviews, the *Los Angeles Times* sounded a sour note. "The bloom is off the Rosen," wrote Leonard Feather, in a brief review. "A Jewish accent and a series of ad lib volleys, no matter how admirably carried out, no longer seem as brilliant per se."[23] Were gags and moments of explosive brilliance going to be enough? Was this simply a matter of relying on past glories? It's perhaps noteworthy that the 2,013-year-old man, as he is in this recording, wants to die (although he's embarrassed that he might meet Jesus, whom he paid four drachmas for a cabinet once). Was Brooks, also, wanting to kill him even as he worried he needed him? Torn between relying on old warhorses and trying to move on?

Turns out he needn't have worried. Yes, when the movie was released in 1974, the *Wall Street Journal* groused that it was "an undisciplined mess of a movie with some hilarious bits and sequences."[24] This was indeed a recurring thread in the criticism of the movie, but it was overshadowed by a general consensus that, in the words of Charles Champlin of the *LA Times*, Brooks's "mock-down, knock-down, bawdy, gaudy, hyper-hip burlesque western is irreverent, outrageous, improbable, often as blithely tasteless as a stag night at the Friar's Club and almost continuously funny."[25]

One fascinating and indicative barometer of Brooks's thoughts on the *limits* of bad taste in comedy appeared as a small controversy in the wake of the movie's release. In a letter published in the *New York Times* and then reprinted in *Mental Retardation News*, the father of a child with Down syndrome complained that the *Saddles* character Mongo was insulting. Using language commonly employed at the time, the father, Terry Boyle, wrote that "from the point of view of every organization and every parent who has worked for the acceptance of Mongoloid children and all retarded children in the community, Mel Brooks has committed a grievous offense against humanity." Brooks wrote back to the *Times* saying that the name, as a viewing of the movie fairly supports, is based on the name of the bongo player Mongo Santamaría. "It is outrageous for anyone to believe that the writers of 'Blazing Saddles' would be as cruel, heartless, and unthinking as to allude comically to anyone suffering from Down's syndrome in a film scenario. . . . I have . . . shown [everyone connected with *Blazing Saddles*] the mail that has come in from the parents of children suffering from Down's syndrome. I cannot tell you how heartsick everyone connected with the film feels."[26]

Brooks's suggestion that no one could possibly think he and his *Blazing Saddles* collaborators would make fun of kids with Down syndrome may, given the range of targets the movie does take on, seem disingenuous at first; but his outrage and unhappiness appear to be real, and may remind us that, frequently if not entirely, Brooks's targets are embodied in the very nature of "punching up"—the minority Jew against the Nazis, the establishment, the cowboys, the Hollywood icons. Yes, he dresses as a Native American; but he doesn't make fun of them, not the way he attacks the cowboys. The same with Cleavon Little and his family. *Essence* magazine got it: they called *Blazing Saddles* "the definitive put-down of stereotyping. What more need you say about a western whose opening scene has the Black laborers sing Cole Porter's *I Get a Kick Out of You* while the evil whites jump up and down ridiculously, singing 'De Camptown Ladies.' . . . *Blazing Saddles is* the movie to see—and bring a bigot!"[27] The storied African-American newspaper the *Chicago Defender* noted that "fallacies other than Western myths are bludgeoned into obscurity. 'Relevant' fallacies, including those that combine to make up a nation's racial stereotypes, are show-cased as the idiotic things they are. Bludgeoning on that order is decidedly redeeming."[28] Many years later, Barack Obama told Brooks that when he was a kid he was "thrilled with the pic-ture" for suggesting that it was possible for a black man to be a sheriff in the United States.[29]

A number of critics compared the movie—and Brooks—unfavorably to Woody Allen, whose *Sleeper* had opened just a few months before; and the actress Hedy Lamarr, whose name is the basis of a running joke throughout the film, sued Brooks for ten million dollars.[30] But *Blazing Saddles* became a massive popular success, the highest grossing film of 1974. Brooks's next picture, *Young Frankenstein*, released late in the year, was fourth, making him a legitimate box-office sensation—although, of course, especially compared with Allen, largely behind the camera.

Gene Wilder, who'd worked with both—Allen had directed him romancing a sheep in *Everything You Always Wanted to Know About Sex* (*But Were Afraid to Ask)*—put it this way: "The way Woody makes a movie, it's as if he were lighting ten thousand safety matches to illuminate a city. Each one of them is a little epiphany—topical, ethnic, or political. What Mel wants to do is to set off atomic bombs of laughter. Woody will take a bow and arrow or a hunting rifle and aim it at small, pre-cise targets. Mel grabs a shotgun, loads it with fifty pellets, and points it in the general direction of one enormous target. Out of fifty, he'll score at least six or seven huge bull's eyes, and those are what people always remember about his films."[31] So Wilder knew what he was in for when he came up with Brooks's next project.

Brooks had announced *Young Frankenstein* even before *Blaz-ing Saddles* came out, even while it was still called *Black Bart*: "Doesn't everyone want to do a take-off of a monster movie?" he told the *New York Times* in 1973.[32] Wilder had done some rewriting on Brooks's projects as early as *The Producers*—reworking some of his lines, improving the scenes—and came to Brooks during shooting on *Blazing Saddles* with a synopsis and introductory scene for another movie, this one based on their shared love of Universal horror films.[33]

Indeed what strikes the lover of film first about *Young Frankenstein* is its incredibly precise production values; Brooks has come a long way from the technical "crudity" of *The Producers*. And that preciseness is employed in the name of fidelity: camera setups, props, lighting, and of course filming in black and white all hew remarkably to the original cinematic source material, even using some of the actual parts of the laboratory set from the original movie and hiring the original builder, who came out of semi-retirement at seventy-seven when Brooks "visited his monster gadget collection and said, 'I want it all.'"[34] (It might be worth pointing out that Brooks and company were closer, chronologically, to the Universal material than we are to *Blazing Saddles*; and that Brooks, of course, had spent the formative years of his career working in black and white, on *Your Show of Shows* and even the pilot of *Get Smart*.) The movie's cinematographer wrote in an article for a trade magazine that *Young Frankenstein* "incorporated more photographic and special effects than any other film I've ever worked on"; with the budget he needed, Brooks was able to create the precise canvas on which he could spread his message of faithful fidelity that would, in turn, allow for the parodic message to run riot.[35]

That said, the preciseness of that canvas at times allowed for a "static and verbal approach" to dominate, as a *Washington Post* reviewer suggested, to rely on the shortcuts provided by the shared aspects of narrative and image "to get them through a rambling collection of scene parodies and a more or less constant stream of puns, double entendres and other verbal rib-pokers and thigh-slappers."[36] Brooks's moves on *Young Frankenstein* are unquestionably familiar to his viewers, including the idea of sublimating any genre to show business, as when Dr. Frankenstein takes his monster and does a twosome of "Puttin' on the Ritz." This is simultaneously an autobiographical reminiscence (as Brooks used to reduce a childhood friend to tears doing something similar), a tip to another movie (where, having captured King Kong, the only thing to do with a monster is make him the basis of a big show), and also, for film fans, an interesting subversion of Peter Boyle, an actor then best known for playing a different kind of monster, a lunchbucket conservative in *Joe*, in 1970.[37] (Boyle would shake his head at the positive responses he got for that role: "A bigot, a killer, becomes a national hero. Where are the people at?")[38] Brooks once more is suggesting that everything, in the end, is fodder for the showbiz maw. "There are vaudeville jokes which may be older than Mary Wollstonecraft Shelley herself," one critic noted.[39]

Brooks also rehearsed his penchant for presenting oversexualized women. Madeline Kahn had burned up the screen in *Blazing Saddles* in an Oscar-nominated Marlene Dietrich-esque turn, singing a Brooks-written song, "I'm Tired," that broadly winked and nodded at the hidden strata of sex work that lay beneath the female characters who populated the saloons and hotels of traditional Western films and TV shows. ("I've had my fill of love/From below and above . . . let's face it, everything below the waist is kaput.") In *Frankenstein*, she appears in the movie as Dr. Frankenstein's beleaguered and frigid fiancée, who comes into her own after what we might call a Transylvanian Mistake—a sexual experience that converts her to the monster's side after an encounter with his enormous "schwanzstucker," an echo of a similar Kahn and Little sequence in *Blazing Saddles*. The roster of women defined in sexual terms is complete with Teri Garr's Inga, a blithe free spirit of sexual openness ("roll, roll, roll in the hay," she says, guilelessly suiting the action to the word, but not averse to reclaiming the metaphor), and Cloris Leachman's brilliant Frau Blücher, the avatar of the hag—during filming, Leachman accidentally ate the fake wart on her chin at lunch—and an ode to sexual sublimation.[40] "Yes!" she screams, violin in hand, as the Freudian psychodrama reaches its height and she reveals her relationship with Frankenstein's grandfather. "HE WAS—HE WAS—MY BOYFRIEND!"[41] There's brilliance in these gags. The *Times* thought it was Brooks's "funniest, most cohesive comedy to date."[42]

There's a good deal of conceptual coherence there, cavils about the plot notwithstanding; there's a good case to be made, in fact, for those looking at *Young Frankenstein* as a meditation on America, and Brooks's own role as a Jewish-American artist. Brooks himself said of the movie that "the only noticeable Jew is Dr. Frankenstein himself, who is played by Gene Wilder. We didn't play it Jewish, but I think it was there."[43] It was, indeed, for those who cared to look (and on a different occasion, anyway, he would say that "the whole thing is dripping with Jewish humor," which seems closer to the mark).[44]

The movie is, at the most fundamental level, all about identity, rebelling against it, and coming to accept, nay, glory in it. How can a movie not be about acculturation when much of its triumphalism comes in accepting your original name, unchanged, from the old country? At first, it's disguised, a matter of pronunciation rather than word: it's pronounced FrONK-en-steen, Wilder insists. But as the family servant, played by the brilliant Marty Feldman, suggests, insisting on this is as silly as his calling himself Eye-gor: it just won't wash. Of course, the wheel of comedy goes around, and this ironic avatar doesn't have tremendous self-knowledge: in the same exchange, when Wilder suggests he can do something about his hump, Eyegor responds, guilelessly: "What hump?"

Accepting his own past involves also accepting a version of himself that Wilder/Frankenstein/the American Jew has kept hidden for a long time, unless, of course, you happen to be Mel Brooks or Zero Mostel: a loud, angry, boisterous version. In the beginning of the movie—and, to be fair, at certain times throughout—Wilder simmers internally, faced with external pressure. The best is the pas-de-deux of infantilism and minimization played between Wilder and Leachman, when she asks him whether he would like something to drink before bed, and refuses to take no for an answer. One can also imagine Leachman's character as either the Gentile or the Jewish mother, never being stood up to. But then the monster is released: and Wilder can scream and rage and *shtup* Teri Garr's shiksa goddess with abandon.

It's a juicy part, aided, of course, by the fact that Wilder wrote it for himself. As the prime generator of the script, Wilder insisted there was no role for Brooks, the whole thing had to be played straight—and it earned the two of them an Oscar nomination for best adapted screenplay. (It ended up losing to *The Godfather, Part II*.) Both *Blazing Saddles* and *Young Frankenstein* were released in Brooks's *annus mirabilis* of 1974, and so ostensibly competed against each other for awards and nominations. *Blazing Saddles* got nominations for its title song, its editing, and for Kahn as best actress. But the two movies combined to make a ton of money: *Young Frankenstein* remained one of the top ten grossers for the first half of 1975, convincing studios that, as Brooks put it, "funny is money," and was directly responsible for a wide range of investment in artists like Joan Rivers, Steve Martin, Gene Wilder, Marty Feldman, Cheech and Chong, Richard Pryor, and Lily Tomlin. Many of these artists got, or at least were lured with later broken promises of, creative control and even revenue sharing—a phenomenon associated with Allen, but of which Brooks was actually a far higher-profile and arguably more influential example.[45]

Looking to Hollywood's past and using it for your own purposes had not only turned out to be quite lucrative, but propelled Brooks to a new tier of fame: in February 1975 he appeared on the cover of *Newsweek* and was also that month's

Playboy interview, his second one—two tectonic tokens of post-war celebrity.[46] So what next? Looking for another genre to parody—"all I'm doing is reliving the movies I loved as a little boy," he would say—and, perhaps, thinking about how he was known, as the voice, the mouthy, verbal Jew, he decided, in his own way, to parody *that*, in the same vein as the joke about the rabbi who is praised to the skies about all sorts of virtues, who breaks in to say, "And about my modesty you say nothing?"[47] Here, too, one can imagine Brooks saying: "You want to talk about loud? Well, I can do quiet, too. I can do quiet as well as anyone." And thus Mel Brooks's *Silent Movie*.

Technically, the idea wasn't his; it had been suggested to him by a social acquaintance of his, the TV writer Ron Clark. (It was also Clark's idea to have the one word in the picture spoken by Marcel Marceau, the world-famous mime.)[48] But note that auteur-like title, in an increasing age of auteurism. Unlike most directors in the 1970s—including, increasingly, Woody Allen—who were cornering the market by putting their personal stamp on one kind of film, Brooks's parodic, showbizzy consciousness embodied the Jewish chameleonic perspective that had built much of American mass culture: we can do everything, and we can do it for you wholesale, and by Thursday to boot. But instead of the crowd-pleasing ethos of those creators, and Brooks's early days, *Silent Movie*, the work of an established super-success, was clearly a kind of fig to the masses, to the studios, to biting the hand that was now feteing him: *is anyone going to watch this kind of movie?*

Which is, of course, the question that animates the movie itself, the first silent Hollywood comedy since Chaplin's *City Lights*, a movie in the same vein as *The Producers*, about the making of a work of cultural entertainment.[49] (You could say the same thing about *Young Frankenstein* as well, although metaphorically: the monster and the movie are interchangeable, both assembled out of old parts to be reanimated as something vibrant in the now.) Brooks's collection of oddballs with mono-syllabic names—Brooks as Mel Funn, Dom DeLuise as Dom Bell, Marty Feldman as Marty Eggs—clearly owe something to Beckett, that great portrayer of both verbosity and its opposite; it's kind of like if Lucky and Pozzo had relocated to Los Angeles. (Sweetly, Brooks in an interview compared them to his brothers, who had become, variously, a war hero, a chemical company executive, and a fast-food franchise operator: a family reunited and in action together, in Hollywoodland if not in life.)[50] The movie is bright and shiny—and the most of its time, the 1970s—in a way that Brooks's other movies aren't. Cameos include many of the biggest stars of the decade: Burt Reynolds, James Caan, Liza Minnelli, Paul Newman, and, yes, Anne Bancroft all show up, a testament to Brooks's heat and show business pull—which both provides enjoyment and abstracts it at the same time, as the viewer marvels at the backstage machinations required and steps away from the picture's heart, to the extent that it has one.

On one level, one might have thought that given all the criticisms of Brooks as a director who strung together collections of gags, that a silent movie—which, even when it's a masterpiece by Chaplin or Keaton, can be largely that—would have been a natural for his talents.[51] But Brooks is not a great director of slapstick, as it turns out. Is it that its loose kineticism is less his métier than the grand burlesque, that seemingly ramshackle setups don't quite work in the same way as the carefully replicated Busby Berkeley-esque mise-en-scènes of *Blazing Saddles* or, later, *History of the World*? Is it actually that Brooks *does* work best with words, that he needs the verbal energy as a catalyst for the pictures he puts on screen? One would hardly want to overstate the argument that, of all the genres of movie comedy, Jews are underrepresented in silent film and slapstick—Brooks's brief former boss Jerry Lewis would argue the point rather loudly, and so, for that matter, would the brilliant silent work of Sid Caesar, and then there are the *Three Stooges!*—but the great tradition of American Jewish film comedy can just as easily be told through following a judicious combination of physical clowning and verbal dexterity, from the Marx Brothers through Brooks himself through his clowning contemporary Woody Allen (in his early films, at the very least).

Silent Movie got a lot of favorable reviews, but not necessarily raves; although it still took the top slot at the box office, it grossed substantially less than Brooks's previous two monster hits. And some of Brooks's friends and acquaintances in Caesar's circle were offended about his portrayal as a second banana to Brooks in the movie.[52] But it didn't seem to worry audiences who were now tuned in to Brooks, as they were with other 1970s directors, frequently the newly dubbed "hyphenates" like writer-hyphen-directors Woody Allen, Robert Altman, Warren Beatty, Francis Coppola, and Martin Scorsese, to see What He Would Do Next.[53] Brooks was more commercially successful than many of them: in 1977, he won the National Association of Theatre Owners Director of the Year Award, given as an acknowledgment for putting bottoms into movie theater seats as much as, or more than, for aesthetic accomplishment. ("I was delighted, especially so since the N.A.T.O. convention is going to be held in Miami and it'll give me a chance to see my little Jewish mother who lives there," Brooks commented.)[54] Unlike most of them, Brooks was also appearing in his movies as an actor, and, by 1976, he was fifth on the list of Top Ten box-office attractions, behind Robert Redford, Jack Nicholson, Dustin Hoffman, and Clint Eastwood, but ahead of Burt Reynolds.

Apparently, Brooks would call up Reynolds—"Number Six! This is Number Five calling!"—and one can only imagine the glee at the self-described "four foot, six inch, freckle faced person of Jewish extraction" (the height a comic exaggeration; Brooks would then add, "I admit it. All but the extraction") waving proof he was a bigger star than the Gentile sex symbol.[55] But there are stars and stars, and while Brooks was clearly an actor as well as a director, he was hardly a sex symbol. Perhaps the proof of his essential, abiding brand of Jewishness—or, perhaps, his Jewish brand—was a project he was tapped to act in that he didn't direct himself.

Carl Reiner was looking to adapt Avery Corman's 1971 novel *Oh, God!* as a movie, and, Larry Gelbart script in hand, decided to make the Caesar alum sweep complete by tapping Brooks to play the Supreme Being—how far could it be from a two-thousand-year-old man, after all?—and Woody Allen as the earthly zhlub he appears to and asks to serve as his divine messenger. Brooks agreed, but then changed his mind after Allen changed his.[56] The parts eventually went to George Burns and John Denver, and there's a whole dissertation to be written on the way in which the latter's casting shifted the movie from what would certainly have been a central moment in calibrating the internal dynamics of American Jewish comedy to something quite different; a metaphor for the larger American acceptance of a formative Jewish role, not just theologically speaking (as in adding the "Judeo-" in "Judeo-Christian country"), but, more to our point, in terms of show business. You couldn't get any more "real American" in 1977 than John Denver—who, in a pre-premiere interview, described his experience with God in the most goyish, least Tevye-ish way imaginable: "The oneness I feel with the great Creator comes from my own experience in life, and from the places where I spend my quiet time, my meditative hours—outdoors, in the mountains and in the forests."[57] And you can't get any more éminence grise-ier than a would-be 2,000-Year-Old Man Burns, playing up the old Borscht Belt rhythms for all they're worth. (His "so help me, me," as he swears on a Bible in court, is worth the price of admission alone.)

Did Brooks, constantly compared—and mindful of the comparisons—to Allen, feel he would be taking the lesser role of the duo by taking a part he hadn't created and shaped if the other didn't? Gelbart dryly—but perceptively—noted about Brooks's recusal from playing God: "I guess Mel didn't want the demotion."[58] Or was it that what appealed to him was the chance to collaborate with this other great comedian, and without that it was simply another project? Was it that he felt the role was a rehash of the 2,000-Year-Old Man, a step backward? A definition of himself as the crazy old Jew, a movie star, yes, but only a certain kind? It doesn't seem coincidental that the role he assayed next—in his next great parody—was in some ways a rejoinder to Reiner, Reynolds, and even the auteurs: he would cast himself as a romantic lead, and he would take on— for the first time—the work of an auteur as the subject for parody, the director who was in many ways the catalyst for the auteur theory itself, Alfred Hitchcock. And, in doing so, setting a "film record" for auteurism himself, wearing the most hats on any production ever: producer, director, co-writer, title song composer-lyricist, and star. You can't get much more hyphenate than that.[59]

Before releasing *High Anxiety*, Brooks felt it was necessary to let it be known that he had sought the master's approval— shades of earlier in his career with Caesar. "If the picture is a sendup, it's also an act of homage to a great artist," Brooks said. "I'm glad I met him, because I love him." At a San Francisco Film Festival tribute where he showed a rough cut, he said he'd studied Hitchcock's work more than any other director's.[60] Brooks could, of course, have portrayed himself as explicitly Jewish, especially since he decided to examine the psychoanalytic roots of Hitchcock movies by setting it among psychoanalysts. But that would have been too easy, so instead he decided to "play Gentile" and play it straight—and then have the Gentiles disguise *themselves* as a bunch of squabbling American Jews as a plot point. In some ways, it's the inverse of the Jewish identity questions of *Young Frankenstein*; Molly Haskell, in a characteristic review, said the movie was "best described as a compilation film in which famous bits and pieces and visual conceits from the ten most familiar Hitchcock films have been shuffled, cross-bred, rewritten and staged with Jewish punchlines." (Tipping his hat to an earlier generation of Jewish comedians who specialized in complicated, subversive ethnic disguise, we're told the middle initial of Brooks's character, the very WASP-y sounding Richard H. Thorndyke, stands for Harpo.)[61]

Which is part of the point. Disguise in general is a theme of the film, particularly when one takes into account that Brooks and co-star Madeline Kahn are playing a peekaboo game of Judaism even more complicated than usual: since in replicating Hitchockian mores, they're stepping into a world that is Gentile in a very different and much more quotidian way. The Western is always a myth, and horror films are always allegory, and to an audience raised on sound pictures silent films are self-conscious artifice, but Hitchcock films work much more prominently on a wrenching turn from a kind of realism, in which a "real person's" world is turned upside down. Of course, those real people—Jimmy Stewart and Cary Grant and Kim Novak and Doris Day and so forth—are always, always Gentile, and possess all the resources and savoir-faire (even if temporarily distressed) that belonging to America's most privileged echelons allow them. Take even the movie's name. Hitchcock's *Vertigo*, Latin for "whirling," announces its sophisticated, classically oriented bona fides. Brooks's title *High Anxiety*, on the other hand, sounds like a neologism straight out of one of those Presbyterian-impersonating country club strivers ("Oh, we go to the best doctors in Vienna. They diagnosed me with high anxiety. Not just regular anxiety. *High!*") The same applies to the organization his character heads: the Psychoneurotic Institute for the Very, Very Nervous.

This, well, high church anxiety plays out in various moments of comic tension through the movie, perhaps most notably when Brooks's psychologist character, ready to discourse on graphic sexual and scatological terminology at a psycho-analytic conference, is faced with a small child in the audience and forced to use schoolhouse euphemisms. One might well argue that Brooks is—in a scene that plays out with typically Hitchcockian and atypically Brooksian restraint—winkingly rehearsing, in metaphor, the dynamic of his entire oeuvre: taking something serious and covering it in pee-pee and poo-poo. As Brooks himself is, in the movie's parody of *The Birds*, where the birds in question do what comes naturally—or, at least, naturally from the perspective of a New York City dweller who's inevitably had at least one such encounter with a pigeon.

If so, it works; as does the (comparatively) subtler Kahn routine in which she mistakes the grunting and straining sounds of Richard Thorndyke being garroted for a caller attempting to initiate phone intimacies. Kahn's increasingly intrigued responses both confirm and explode the bases of that "Jewish science" of psychoanalysis—not everything is about sex, but, on the other hand, it is. Or, as a critic put it about fifteen years earlier: "I don't know much about psych-analysis, but I'd say this is a dirty picture." Unusually for a Brooks picture, it even has nudity in it; and, even more unusually, it's Brooks himself doing the disrobing, in the movie's most explicit—in every sense—parodic moment of the Hitchcockian oeuvre.

Brooks-as-Thorndyke has previously made a big deal about getting his newspaper to an increasingly aggrieved bellhop (played by co-writer and future *Diner* director Barry Levinson). Settling into his hotel room, Thorndyke then steps into the shower, where—shades of *Psycho*—he is "stabbed" by the bellhop with the newspaper. Its ink swirls down the drain, exactly as the blood does in the original movie. "When people see this," Brooks said about the scene, "I want them to say, 'He may be just a small Jew, but I love him. A short little Hebrew man, but I'd follow him to the ends of the earth.' I want every fag in L.A. to see it and say, 'Willya *look* at that *back?*'"[62] There's camp in

that comment, of course; another complex conflation of gay-
ness and Jewishness and show business (it's the gay population
of Los Angeles that Brooks explicitly includes, after all).[63] But
there's also the desire not just to be admired or laughed at, but
ogled. A surprisingly effective turn where Brooks/Thorndyke
does his best Frank Sinatra impersonation, which turns out to
be very good indeed, both parodies and channels the desire to
have bobby-sox appeal, too; to actually be the crooning idol.[64]
Or, as a showman put it years ago, "And please . . . love . . . Melvin . . . Brooooks!"

Did he love them back? Brooks, in an interview about the
shower scene, noted that in his experience of audiences' reactions the big laugh came early, when he would take off the
robe at the beginning of the scene. "They are saluting the in-
tention of the scene," he would say, giving the audience credit
for being the same as he was: lovers of Hollywood and intuitive
comprehenders of its genres, beats, and iconic moments. In a
moment of quasi-humility, he would say, in a late-in-life interview, "the truth is, 70 or 80 percent of the audience is as bright
as the filmmaker."[65] And the evidence he had was that they loved
his pictures, which required just those skills, along with the same
loves he did. "Hitchcock has noted the difference between surprise and suspense, preferring suspense," one critic noted. "Brooks
manipulates the far broader difference between surprise and
nostalgia, and gets most of his mileage from the latter."[66] In
that sense—in the sense that they shared his approach to Hollywood, to American culture, to America—he had turned them
Jewish, and so they had become *mishpokhe*.

The same year Brooks won the National Association of
Theatre Owners director award, Allen won the Oscar for *Annie
Hall*. The divergence was financial, true; Allen himself said that
Love and Death, *Sleeper*, and *Take the Money and Run* together
didn't match the gross of *Blazing Saddles*.[67] But it was more than
that. Some of the cognoscenti were under the impression that

it was Allen who was the voice of American Jewish comedy; and in some precincts, that was unquestionably the case. But Allen always presented himself—in persona and in his moviemaking choices—as a man apart. In *Annie Hall*, Alvy Singer was famously uncomfortable with Hollywood, dismissing the cultural benefits of California as the ability to make a right turn on red. A man whose movie's original title was *Anhedonia*—the clinical inability to take pleasure from life—Allen presented himself in *Annie Hall* as someone whose personality, and, by not too disguised metaphorical expansion, whose Jewishness, emphasized the gulf, rather than the connection, that his outsider status bestowed.

Brooks, on the other hand, talked about his movies as "potato salad pictures"—"You're in the deli and there's this guy with a little piece of potato salad stuck in the corner of his mouth, and he's talking about your picture to his cronies. He's saying, all the time with potato salad hanging, 'You gotta see this Mel Brooks pitcha, you'll laugh so hard you'll *pish* yourself.'"[68] Not films, not cinema, *pictures:* while Allen was in the process of working on the deals that would give him financial and artistic independence for almost the rest of his career, Brooks, by contrast, was ever more firmly enmeshed in the studio machine, complete with a corner suite in the 20th Century Fox office building, dispensing Raisinets to all and sundry. ("Eat them, eat them, they're good for you. They're nutritious—whatever damage the chocolate is doing, the raisins are correcting.")[69] Granted, the particular niche Brooks was carving out relied on a certain parodic distance; but it was the distance of the court jester. Brooks's parodies of the movies were part of the romance America had with movies, and with its own culture, itself.

But the distance between the two figures was never quite as much as people made it out to be. Allen would compliment Brooks personally, saying he was "*so* nice to me" when they worked together for Caesar, "nice, amusing, intelligent as could be" and that he himself was "a good audience for Mel Brooks . . . I laugh at his pictures."[70] Brooks, for his part, said *Annie Hall* "was the first time in my life that I wanted to write a letter to a film-maker." (He then said when he ran into Allen at a Chinese restaurant and told him so, the response was: "You should have.")[71] And—because Brooks contained multitudes—he wanted to make pictures for the "smarties," too. It may not have hurt that in 1977, the year after Brooks twitted Reynolds for being Number Five, he dropped down to Number Seven on the list of box-office appeal—right behind Woody Allen. (Burt Reynolds could thumb his nose at them both, rising back up to fourth place.)[72] In a 1979 interview with old friend Joseph Heller promoting the latter's book *Good as Gold*, Brooks said, "I've been asked to ask you questions, as a profound West Coast intellectual. There's only three of us."[73] Behind the joke, one can feel the sting of something unhappily unrecognized. And so, his Hollywood clout expanded, he became, yes, a producer.

4

◆ı◆ı◆

Jews in Space, and Time

IF MOSTEL AND WILDER turned the title of producer into a symbol of cynicism and shlock, Brooksfilms was, well, the exact opposite. Brooks the intellectual was the man who said, "My God, I'd love to smash into the casket of Dostoevsky, grab that bony hand, and scream at the remains, 'Well done, you goddam genius!'" He used the company to create films that fulfilled his "need to describe things of a more exquisite and subtle nature . . . to convey my own more muted and complicated passions," but he understood that his reputation and brand wouldn't quite allow him to be seen as taking a personal touch. Or, as he put it: "I knew the critics would take offense if there was a property they felt was sacred and the bean-farting wacko from *Blazing Saddles* was going to put his grimy paws on it."[1]

Not that there weren't *any* personal touches: the new production company's first film, *Fatso*, was put together in no small part in order to let Bancroft direct, and it starred Brooks favorite Dom DeLuise.[2] And although one of its biggest commercial and critical successes, *My Favorite Year*, had started out as a story about Wyatt Earp and the publicist trying to keep him reined in while he promoted his memoir in New York, it changed—in part because it was considered a possible vehicle for Brooks—to revolve around a young comedy writer, a Caesar-like figure, and a live show during the early days of television.[3]

But many of the movies that came out under the Brooks-films banner were less *heymish*—unless you take the "dress British, think Yiddish" dictum as your guide, as in some ways Brooks did. Many of the productions displayed more than a little touch of Anglophilia, the American intellectual's sigil and shield (*The Elephant Man, 84 Charing Cross Road*); or cultivated particular auteurs and visions that took movie staples to places they had never been before, but in a more surrealist, experimental key—the Ernie Kovacs to Brooks's own Sid Caesar. Brooks, for example, tapped David Cronenberg to direct *The Fly* and gave David Lynch a job with *Elephant Man*—which co-starred Bancroft—after seeing his unclassifiable horror movie *Eraserhead*. Brooks would often call Lynch "Jimmy Stewart from Venus," which was a compliment, but hardly gives the sense of a fellow neighbor of the shtetl.[4] All of these films—in one way or another—reflected the producer's love of cinema, his unwillingness to rest easy. "Maybe it's part of the whole Jewish thing," Brooks mused at the time. "'I pledge two dollars anonymous for the crippled children.' It makes you feel good when you do something like that."[5]

In this sense, Brooks modeled another rising American Jewish movie mogul at the turn of the 1980s. Steven Spielberg had made his monstrous splash around the same time as Brooks's commercial successes, with the 1975 blockbuster *Jaws*. Another movie brat who shifted in a protean way between genre and cultural register, Spielberg may have been a defter hand behind the camera than Brooks—it's hard to imagine anyone contesting the point—but his move in the '80s to take on less genre-oriented material like *Empire of the Sun* and *The Color Purple* followed a similar dynamic of "being taken seriously." In both cases, the opposition of whether popular and populist filmmakers should be dowered with the same recognition that auteurist favorites were can be correlated with the question of whether there was, in some sense, a glass ceiling for a certain kind of Jewish entry into the most privileged and sacrosanct echelons of cultural custodianship.

That question, put more bluntly in the form "Will Spielberg ever get a best director Oscar?" was rarely if ever posed in Brooks's case, perhaps because the answer was so "obvious." The three films Brooks was more deeply involved in during the 1980s were ambitious, too, but in quite another direction than Spielberg—reaching, in their own way, through time and space, and struggling, in many ways more explicitly than the works of the '70s, with depicting Jewishness, and particularly Jewish history, on screen. (Spielberg, of course, would do the same in the 1990s, which finally won him that best-director Oscar.)

The first was *History of the World, Part I*, released in 1981. Continuous with the now-established Brooks brand, it parodied film genres, in this case, a mash-up of several: the historical epic, the Bible film, and the anthology film. This last was a particularly useful response to the general critique of Brooks's movies as plotless, just a bunch of gags: no one expects a sustained plot in an anthology, and Brooks certainly didn't oblige. Bancroft, describing the appeal of the picture to her husband, said: "he can play any period in which he feels happy." Brooks, addressing his leading role through the ages, said: "It was a Mel Brooks concept, therefore wouldn't it be proper if Mel Brooks were in every episode, to give it a unity that the different chapters need?"[6] The sustained set-piece nature of several of the settings, though—the Stone Age, ancient Rome, the French

Revolution—allowed the opportunity for Brooks to think through the ramifications of a historical period, rather than simply its second-hand Hollywood version.

All too frequently, it was an opportunity Brooks was unwilling or unable to rise to; preferring, instead, to indulge his penchant for his favorite habits. That said, certain moments had an unexpected, perhaps sometimes unplanned, depth. There were the Hollywood in-jokes, like Hugh Hefner's appearance as a sybarite. Which, to be fair, had something to say about the historical resonance of 1970s outré decadence in the entertainment industry. (About Madeline Kahn's reappearance as the Empress Nympho, another in her line of Brooks's women defined by sexual behaviors, we pass over near-silently.) Brooks's role as Comicus, the "stand-up philosopher," deflated at the unemployment office by Bea Arthur—"Oh, a bullshit artist!" she calls him—says more about Brooks's take on the intellectualism debate the press had been waging between him and Woody Allen than any manifesto he could have possibly made. To be fair, the protagonists didn't actually disagree: Allen had been saying in interviews he was a bullshitter for years. But no one believed him. (Brooks, in a personal essay about the movie, said of Comicus, "I am living proof that bad jokes never die; they just find their way from one civilization to the other." Which can also serve in place of a manifesto.) And, finally, there's the reference back to his own personal history, presenting Comicus, according to Brooks, as a tribute to his idol Eddie Cantor, and of course Caesar, in the Stone Age skit, as the evolutionary Father, creating Art.[7]

The Art in question is urinated on by a Stone Age critic; and it wasn't the only place in the movie Brooks indulged his predilection for scatology, retelling the prince and pauper story in the French Revolution scene, but with a piss-boy replacing the pauper. And it's hard to find a better return on puerile investment than in Brooks's rendition of the Last Supper, in which a meal is made around the fact that we now say "Jesus" as a mild oath, with a kind of "Who's on First" routine that could have been at home on *Your Show of Shows*—except that back then the Lord's name would never have crossed the lips of anyone on the airwaves, of course.

Brooks's role in that "Last Supper" skit—both as Comicus turned exasperated Jewish waiter and as writer-director—recasts one of the most sacred of Christian moments and, in Leonardo da Vinci's representation, one of the most iconic of Christian visuals, as a Jewish product. That said, the scene ends, ultimately, as a subordinate homage to that painting; everyone budges up when Leonardo arrives and gets into their proper New Testamental order. Comicus, by means of his tray, even provides the halo for John Hurt's Jesus, simultaneously profaning and sacralizing.

But as we've seen before, Brooks ultimately worships a different god, one that his Jewishness, essential as it is, is subordinated to. There's a hint of it early in the movie, when Brooks's Moses sacrifices a third of God's commandments for the sake of a joke, and in order to make sure the show goes on. (He started out with fifteen commandments, but then five of them drop and break.) This could have been a 2,000-Year-Old Man sequence, and sounds like it: "Fifteen—Ten! Ten Commandments!" But the same can by no means be said for the most audacious, and brilliant, sequence in the film, in which Jewishness itself, or, at least, Jewish history, is thrown out entirely. Or, perhaps better put, is subject to an inquisition.

To misquote Monty Python's Flying Circus, no one expects the Spanish Inquisition in a comedy by an American Jewish icon; although if you were going to, it would be in one by the guy who made the comedy about Nazis. And at first glance, it would be simple enough to suggest this was a medieval page torn from Brooks's *Producers* playbook, suggesting, in turning the Inquisition's torture chambers into the backdrop for an Esther Williams aquatic showcase—which cost more than *The Producers'* entire budget—that the way to get rid of threats to Jews is to ridicule them.[8]

But is that exactly what's going on? It's true, the Inquisition looms large in Jewish history, and memory; but generally speaking it hardly pushed the same buttons as swastikas and goose-stepping did in the late 1960s. What the idea of the Inquisition contributed to the contemporary American Jewish discourse was less its specter of violence than its resonances of conversion—here, as opposed to the medieval Iberian peninsula, in a cultural sense rather than a confessional one. And who was the converter in chief? Mel Brooks himself, dressed as Torquemada.

It's actually one of his great acting performances. Brooks exudes a kind of raffish charm, suggesting that, despite the surrounding settings, he's actually kind of a good guy. His delivery of the line defining an auto-da-fé—"it's what you ought not to do but you do anyway"—is a classic, suggesting the temptations of giving in, of letting something burn. Precisely what might be hinted at in the particular way he addresses his Jewish captives strung up on the walls. (We know they're Jewish, because one of them is Jackie Mason.)

TORQUEMADA: Confeeeessss—don't be booooooring.
 Say yeeeesss—don't be dull
 A fact—you're ignoring
 It's better to lose your skullcap than your skull!
CAPTIVES: Oy-yoy-gevalt!

In other words, the biggest crime of traditional Jewishness is not theological devotion or traditional observance—how could it be, in America, in the year of not particularly or necessarily our lord 1981? For Brooks, the biggest crime of the World of His Fathers was gravity and dullness. All those sepia-toned Roman Vishniac historical Jewish portraits had gotten it right:

Jewishness was black and white. And Torquemada's the one in brilliant, tailored, showbizzy red.

Years before, Brooks had suggested that Bancroft didn't need to convert because she was a star; well, now he was a star, too, and he'd conquered American movie comedy, reshaped it in his (okay, maybe his and Allen's, and pre-*Ishtar*, you could add Elaine May's) image. What more did he need? *History of the World, Part I*, ended with coming attractions for a putative Part II. One scene from the purported sequel features an ice-skating Hitler; another, Jews in space. ("They're going to protect the Hebrew race!") On the one hand, one could take this as a sign of Brooks's constant preoccupation with these topics, and an insistence on the eternal verities of Jewish humor, even into the science-fiction future. In an interview a few years earlier, as *High Anxiety* was in post-production, he said that "because of the success of *Star Wars* my next movie will be 'Galactic Mishegoss,' the story of three Jews shot into space on a six-pointed rocket ship on a trip underwritten by a kosher wine company. Of course, it'll be the basis for a TV series titled 'Space Rabbi.'"[9]

In other words, the whole joke relied on the idea that the movie was never going to be made. "If Part I grosses $100 million, there will definitely be a part II," he said in an interview, but that was more a calculated dismissal in advance—even his blockbusters had never made anything close to that—and borne out thumpingly by the facts. *History of the World, Part I* got mixed reviews at best.[10] Critics objected to the recycling of jokes, to the bad taste, the usual litany—it was just that here the balance outweighed the countervailing assessments of brilliance. "Uneven Mel Brooks epic comedy," *Variety* toplined it, which, along with the *LA Times* headline "The Formula Turns Sour," said it all. Box office followed the critics, as well as bad word of mouth.[11] Nonetheless, Brooks still shared, or said he did, the same sentiment his character expressed in the movie—"It's good to be the king"—and really, anything that opened in theaters against Spielberg's *Raiders of the Lost Ark* was going to suffer by comparison.[12] (Besides, he said, the international receipts, by the terms of his deal, earned him 18 million dollars.) Assuredly Brooks didn't need Indiana Jones to tell him that hating Nazis could be good business. And that would be the focus of his next work: which wrapped together anti-Semitism, Jewish history, and Jewish show business history, in the remake of a film classic.

The original *To Be or Not to Be* was a nuclear explosion of mid-century Jewish comic talent, with two very different members of the pantheon brought together in the crucible of war. Ernst Lubitsch was an émigré who'd fled Europe as Nazism loomed large on the horizon to create comedies with a famously light touch and a cosmopolitan sensibility. Jack Benny was the vastly famous radio comedian—his voice was the most recognized in America in the 1940s, beating out FDR's—whose Jewishness was both rarely apparent and, at least to those in the know, omnipresent on his show. (Brooks would say that growing up, "we all knew that Jack Benny was Jewish.")[13] His stinginess, his shnookdom, and of course his self-deprecating comic timing all came together in the iconic two-line bit when "Benny" is held up by robbers:

ROBBER: Your money or your life!
(Long pause. So long you begin to wonder whether Benny has forgotten his next line, were it not for the explosions of laughter.)
BENNY (*finally*): I'm thinking! I'm thinking!

All this read as Jewish to those in the know. But when Lubitsch and Benny came together to craft the 1942 story of a brilliant, dizzying escapade of Shakespeare and spycraft in Nazi-occupied Poland, where a vain actor and his daring scene partner, who happens to be his wife, get caught up in helping the Free Polish forces, the comic stakes were far different, and more intense, than in Brooks's *The Producers*, released a quarter-century later. In Lubitsch's movie, Benny plays a Pole, not a Jew. But there is a clearly Jewish character, Greenberg, who at a crucial moment in the movie distracts some Nazis by reciting from a different Shakespeare play than the one the troupe is playing and that gives the movie its title. Greenberg quotes Shylock—and that story, and its image of the persecuted Jew, rings loudly at a time when filmgoers might not have known precisely what was happening to the Jews of Poland, but they definitely knew it wasn't anything good.

In a debate between critic and artist that had uncanny echoes when Brooks released *The Producers* in 1967, the *Times* reporter Bosley Crowther wrote that "perhaps there are plenty of persons who can overlook the locale, who can still laugh at Nazi generals with pop-eyes and bunglesome wits," but that "to say [the film] is callous and macabre is understating the case . . . too bad a little more taste and a little more unity of mood were not put in this film. As it is, one has the strange feeling that Mr. Lubitsch is a Nero, fiddling while Rome burns."[14] Given the wartime context, Crowther also seemingly implied that minimizing the Nazi menace through comedy might even undermine the Allied efforts against the Axis forces. Lubitsch himself was given an entire column to respond to those critics who "apparently like the picture but don't seem to be quite sure if they did the right thing in enjoying it."

"How about my taste—or rather my lack of taste?" Lubitsch first asks, answering that his "co-defendant" in the charge is "the American motion-picture audience," who themselves have excellent taste: "I have never yet seen a vulgarity or an off-color joke getting a chance with a motion-picture audience." While there, at least in the general point, Lubitsch and Brooks might well disagree, it is in the critics' identification of that vulgarity with laughing during the film itself that Lubitsch zeroes in on:

> Aren't they aware of what happened to Poland? Did I try to make them look at the Polish background through rose-colored glasses? Nothing of the kind. I went out of my way to remind them of the destruction of the Nazi conquest, of the terror regime of the Gestapo. . . . Never once have they laughed at the expense of Poland or the Polish people. They have laughed at actors. . . . Do I really picture the Nazis so harmless that it might be a dangerous misleading of the American people by making them underestimate the enemy? . . . No, the American audiences don't laugh at those Nazis because they underestimate their menace, but because they are happy to see this new order and its ideology being ridiculed.[15]

Lubitsch articulates, in ways Brooks himself did over and over again, the essential savvyness of the audience in understanding motion pictures—crucial for understanding what Lubitsch calls his "new recipe" for "a tragical farce or a farcical tragedy," and just as much so for understanding Brooks's groundbreaking parodies. But even more importantly, he suggests the same comic ethos of linking seemingly offensive comedy to moral consciousness, caricature to ethical ridicule.[16] (Recall, also, Brooks's ambitions in *Blazing Saddles*, also self-proclaimed in later interviews, to take on racism.) But there was also a way in which Lubitsch, whose rebuttal largely triumphs, is not a complete victory, in part because he fails to encompass within it the picture's whole achievement. It's true, Benny and company (spoiler alert!) succeed in their particular mission. But *To Be or Not to Be*, original version, is not only about comedy's successes, but also about its failures: about the necessity of replacing theater with action, although theatrics can, and do, help. This tension was always going to be at the heart of Brooks's remake of the film.

It should be said that Brooks neither wrote nor directed the movie, though he worked on the script, directed individual moments, and was involved in the editing.[17] Given the fact that it was a remake, with script and directorial template already available, the necessity for directing must have loomed less large for Brooks, who—like Allen, for that matter—frequently characterized his need to direct as a protective one, to safeguard the intent and effect of the writing from another person's interference.[18] It would also allow him to focus on his performance, which would be a significant challenge on many fronts: he was stepping into the shoes of one of his personal comic heroes, to whom he would automatically be compared. (Allen, to whom he'd been compared so frequently, was somewhere between a peer and a member of a younger generation—he'd been wet behind the ears on *Caesar's Hour* when Brooks was already an established TV writing heavyweight, and Brooks affectionately referred to him as "a little red-headed rat.")[19] Unlike most of Brooks's roles in his own movies, his role here was a sustained character effort, requiring a continuity of acting focus he'd required himself to do less of in his gag-oriented productions. And, of course, he was acting across from a world-class actress: one he happened to be married to.

The remake rights to Benny's movie belonged to a high school friend of Bancroft's, who thought the duo would be great together.[20] Although they'd briefly worked together off and on over the years—Brooks had written for a Bancroft television special, "Annie, the Women in the Life of a Man," which won her an Emmy in 1970, and had guest-starred in another special in 1974, "Annie and the Hoods"—Brooks's public partnerships with his wife had been limited. In an interview around the time of "Annie and the Hoods," he said that "the only reason that he has never performed with his wife before is that he never got around to it. 'Oh, we've done things together at parties, like singing harmony on a couple of songs—'Nothing Could be

Finer . . . Carolina in the Morning,' 'People Will Say We're in Love.' But this is the first time we've worked together professionally."[21] Did Brooks feel more comfortable working with his wife on-camera, in the *Silent Movie* scene and now here across an entire picture, as his own star rose to equal, or even eclipse, hers? Whatever the reason, Bancroft's old friend was right: they *were* great together. Their sequence dancing together to a Polish version of "Sweet Georgia Brown," full of energy and chemistry, is one of the movie's genuine moments (the inclusion of singing and dancing is one of the few truly original aspects of the remake). But the film, in many ways, feels particularly airless.

In part, this stemmed from changing historical consciousness among Americans and American Jews, and the moral consequences that came with it. Brooks's *To Be or Not to Be* was released just four years after the airing of the television mini-series *Holocaust* in 1979, starring (among others) Meryl Streep, which has been often credited with stirring a new awareness of—and reckoning with—the Nazis' war against the Jews, not just against the Allies. It was also just six years after the Supreme Court decided the case of *National Socialist Party of America v. Village of Skokie*. Catalyzed by neo-Nazis' desire to march in the village, the decision reaffirmed the country's commitment to free speech—even speech considered vulgar, blasphemous, and offensive, something Brooks knew more than a little about—while simultaneously acknowledging the strains of white supremacism and anti-Semitism still current in America, something Brooks was also certainly mindful of.

"Has anybody read that Nazis are going to march in New Jersey?" Woody Allen alter ego Isaac Davis asks in the 1979 film *Manhattan*. "We should go down there, get some bricks and baseball bats and really, y'know, explain things to them." Told by one of his fellow conversationalists that "there was this devastating satirical piece on that in the op-ed page of the *New*

York Times," Davis responds, "Well, a satirical piece in the *New York Times* is one thing, but bricks and baseball bats really gets right to the point." Challenged—"*Really* biting satire is always better than physical force"—Davis doubles down: "No, physical force is always better with Nazis, because, uh, it's hard to satirize a guy with shiny boots on." Antithetical to Brooks's whole approach—whose anti-Nazi satirical thrust takes formative shape, in no small part, from the show-business-like shininess of those boots and uniforms—Allen's point here, the squirm-inducing nature of much of the rest of the movie notwithstanding, resonates now, in the days after Charlottesville and renewed debate over punching Nazis.[22] Brooks's *To Be or Not to Be*, on the other hand, has almost entirely fallen off the radar.

It's possible to suggest that Brooks, in shifting his attentions from the Nazis to something closer to the Holocaust, felt the necessity to leaven *The Producers'* comic tension and outrageousness with some kind of dignity and responsibility. (Brooks himself would say in 2011, asked about *Springtime for Hitler:* "It's not the Holocaust. *Springtime for Hitler* is about making fun of Hitler and his dreams of conquering the world.")[23] Brooks's remake is far more explicitly Jewish than its predecessor; it explicitly discusses Jewish victims of Nazism, which Lubitsch's film did not. (Lubitsch doesn't mention Jews anywhere in that *New York Times* rebuttal either, uncomfortably reminding us of that paper's—and the American press's—slowness and silence in reporting on the genocide of European Jewry.) In that culminating monologue by Greenberg in Benny's film, Lubitsch replaced any explicit Jewish reference (such as "Hath not a Jew eyes?") by saying "we" instead. "Have we not eyes?" Greenberg says, and the literal context of the scene would clearly suggest that the pronoun refers to Poles in general, not Jews in particular. Brooks, by contrast, restores the original reference. The movie also makes space for representation of another group of Nazi victims: in contrast to many of Brooks's earlier movies, the re-make contains a non-stereotyped representation of a gay man.[24]

And yet Brooks also plays Hitler himself, in another change from the original movie. Given Brooks's longtime love of im-personating the dictator—ever since he was actually fighting against him in World War II—the temptation must have been irresistible. (He had dental problems throughout the shoot and "more than once interrupted takes to rush to a dentist in his Hitler costume.")[25] But, for the sake of the film, it probably should have been resisted. That Brooksian wink, that intrusion of another meta-level of artifice—*look, Ma, it's me, playing Hit-ler in a picture!*—jarred with the tense comic premise of the rest of the film. Brooks's mustaches became too inconsequential for the task of portraying the inconsequentiality they were trying for. Kevin Thomas, reviewing the movie for the *Los Angeles Times*, struck to the heart of the matter: noting how "we know far more than was known in 1942 of the full extent of the Nazi evil, especially in regard to the fate of the Jews," he felt Brooks's buffoonish Nazism, when "we know full well that the peril of Brooks's largely Jewish acting company is all too real, isn't very funny but instead is merely crass. Ironically, for all its sparkle, the original actually took the Nazis far more seriously than this remake does."[26]

The critics were fairly united in their generally positive if somewhat tepid response; the audience stayed away—certainly compared to Brooks's recent run—and the commercial troubles would extend to Brooksfilms as well, with the critical, commer-cial, and costly failure of the 1986 science-fiction film *Solar-babies.*[27] The longtime Brooks supporter and hugely successful producer Alan Ladd, Jr.—whose science-fiction cred was well established in the industry since he'd championed a largely or-phaned film in production called *Star Wars*—asked him why he was mucking around with the real thing when he could be doing a parody. Why not take those Jews in space, Brooks mused, and make them into a full-length feature after all?[28]

And thus 1987's *Spaceballs* (original title: *The Planet Moron*), a long midrash on those dancing Hasidim in the spacecraft shaped like the Star of David at the end of *History of the World, Part I*, and a fulfillment of its essential thesis: Jews have always been with us, and they always will be. That is, at least, insofar as they conform precisely to our current comic stereotypes. If on its release *Blazing Saddles* was hailed in some precincts, not least Black ones, as a triumph against stereotyping, no one would possibly make that claim about *Spaceballs*, where the American Jewish stereotypes come fast and furious—or, depending on your perspective, slowly and painfully. Although George Lucas's movie's genealogy is as goyish as it gets—he based it in no small part on Flash Gordon, a polo-playing Yalie, for goodness sake—the ingénue in *Spaceballs* is a, um, Druish princess (who is threatened with the return of her original nose, and about whom the line is actually spoken, "Funny, you don't look Druish"). Dark Helmet, rather than a tall, imposing figure voiced by James Earl Jones—an original choice for *Tex X*—is played by the Canadian Jewish comic actor Rick Moranis, and the original's unforgettable heavy breathing is explained via good old Jewish bronchial insufficiency. Pride of place belongs to Brooks himself, duded up in full Yoda outfit and reminding us that the Schwartz flows through us all—that Brooks's Jewish humor, in other words, has captured American dad humor, American dirty jokes, and American film parody all in one.

And Yogurt (as the character is called in the film) is also a Jewish *hondler*, another in the occasional series of figures going all the way back to the 2,000-Year-Old Man who was in the Jewish star-making business; he's fascinated—obsessively so—with how the *Star Wars* franchise has become more than just a series of movies but a business monolith, repurposed and transformed and commodified into all sorts of incredibly unlikely things. Meeting Yogurt for the first time, the heroes ask him: "What is this place? What do you do here?" Yogurt, in his Brooklyn accent, rasps: "Moichandising!" explaining the concept by revealing a Spaceballs gift shop. "We put de name of de picture on everything! Moichandising! Where de *real* money from de movie is made!"

Famously, Lucas's billions came in no small part from a negotiation where he kept the merchandising rights to *Star Wars* when the studio couldn't see any possible value in them; but Brooks is particularly insistent on the idea, so common now, of the merchandising material being the tail wagging the cinematic dog. "Spaceballs—the T-shirt! Spaceballs—the coloring book! Spaceballs—the lunchbox! Spaceballs—the breakfast cereal! Spaceballs—the flamethrower! The kids love this one . . . And last, but not least, Spaceballs—the doll! Me. [He squeezes the doll and pulls a string, a squeaky "May de Schwartz be with you" comes out] Isn't he adorable?" And the cast smiles and nods; Mel Brooks, again, has presented himself for the audience's love, this time in merchandisable, huggable, lovable doll form. And he got it, though only partially in the way he might have expected: especially since in his discussions with George Lucas, Lucas was, in Brooks's words, "going to be a good sport" about Brooks's satire, but he "had one major concern—and a legitimate one. Which was, if we're going to satirize his movies, that we weren't going to merchandize anything from the film. And that's all right with us."[29]

With one quasi-exception. In a particularly inspired bit, Dark Helmet finds out his nemeses' whereabouts by pulling out the already-completed videocassette of the movie and fast-forwarding to the relevant scene. To find it, a subordinate officer, and the camera, track through a long line of tapes of all of Brooks's other films—the movie's *real* merchandising ploy, reminding us, or, in the case of new fans like I was at the time, informing us, that the movie we're watching is the latest iteration in a particular brand, available, of course, for rental or purchase now, thanks to the newly available technology of home video. No need to wait for the television movie of the week or the beneficence of a local second-run theater; now, if you so choose, you could have all Brooks, all the time.

Video became an important part of his fortunes, especially as *Spaceballs* received a generally negative critical response and continued Brooks's streak of significantly underperforming his string of box-office successes in the 1970s; home rentals, and home viewing on cable, helped significantly to ensure the movie's profitability, and his continued relevance and profile.[30] It's probably worth noting that this was the first of Brooks's parodies whose catalytic impulse didn't come from his own childhood viewing and interests; instead, as he acknowledged in interviews, it stemmed from his son's affection for the genre. "Me, they're not my favorites," he said. And: "Listen, the kids know all these movies by heart, so we're going with the force."[31] In many ways, this explains the focus of *Spaceballs* on its existence as a product, and prefigured Brooks's next act: as a commodifier and a repurposer and seller of his older hits and older shtick.

Spaceballs wasn't Brooks's final film outing. He directed three films in the early 1990s, which will get, perhaps deservedly, shorter shrift here. In *Life Stinks* (1991), Brooks plays a heartless CEO who agrees to live on the streets as a homeless person for thirty days on a bet and learns lessons about life and love while doing so. The movie was the director's, as opposed to Brooksfilms's, bid for a serious statement. It hoped to approach the feel of the Preston Sturges classic comedy *Sullivan's Travels*, in which a Depression-era film director noted for his light comedies wants to switch gears and make serious movies about the plight of the poor, going "undercover" as a hobo in order to do so. (The planned film is called *O Brother, Where Art Thou?* a title the Coen brothers, the American Jewish filmmakers who were just beginning to develop their own voice at the time, snagged for their own movie a decade or so after *Life Stinks* came out.)

In the Sturges movie, Sullivan learns his lesson: after a series of travails including loss of memory and being sentenced to six years at hard labor, he understands he's best suited for—and most helpful to his audience when—making light comedies. (His revelation comes from watching his fellow prisoners roaring with laughter at a Walt Disney cartoon.) Brooks—a Depression-era kid, remember, who would have seen the movie as a teenager—was clearly exploring the question that had weighed on him through the '80s: whose lesson to learn, Sturges's or Sullivan's? Stay in the same gear? Or make a film that dramatizes the filmmaker's tension? Ultimately, though, his audience gave him the answer, painfully; the reviews were heavily negative and the box office was abysmal.[32] Stick to Sullivan, they seemed to be saying.

It may not be irrelevant to note that *Life Stinks* is probably Brooks's least Jewish movie to date. While Sturges himself was to the manor almost born—he was adopted by a wealthy stockbroker as a small child and spent most of his childhood in France—and thus finds a comfortable analogue in the blithe Sullivan, Brooks's character, who, unlike Sturges, he plays as well as directs, is deeply unlike him. The catalyzing bet is between Brooks's character and Jeffrey Tambor's; but it's Brooks who plays the rich man's son, and Tambor the up-from-nothing striver. Brooks's character even tries to find genuine support and succor from a church! It's an uncomfortable suit of clothes for Brooks to be trying on; and it doesn't fit well. Of course he was creating the film from a position of incredible success, and it's understandable to imagine why he saw himself as the CEO; but his American Jewish success is of a very different sort, and so the lessons it teaches and provides are different from the ones *Life Stinks* tries, and largely fails, to offer.

Wounded from the response to *Life Stinks*, Brooks, like

Sullivan, retreated to his most successful métier, the genre parody, and to a particular sub-genre he'd never quite gotten his teeth into: the Robin Hood story. He had been a fan since the beginning: Errol Flynn's *The Adventures of Robin Hood* was released at the perfect age for him, with its male derring-do and blazing Technicolor designed to knock the socks off a twelve-year-old. Brooks had been thinking about Robin Hood professionally at least since the days of the 2,000-Year-Old Man (who had, as you recall, described the character as stealing from the rich and keeping it for himself, but had his reputation repaired by a great press agent). In the wake of his successes with *Blazing Saddles* and *Young Frankenstein*, he'd actually co-created a parody TV series based on the Robin Hood stories, *When Things Were Rotten* (lyric from the theme song: "They laughed, they loved, they fought, they drank/They jumped a lot of fences/They robbed the rich, gave to the poor/Except what they kept for expenses"). As with *Get Smart*, Brooks was involved in conceiving the show, casting, and the pilot, but not much after that; unlike *Get Smart*, the show didn't run very long; it was killed by the network after thirteen episodes, despite decent ratings.[33]

After *History of the World, Part I*, Brooks had announced that his next project would be a Robin Hood movie, but that version, planning to star *Young Frankenstein*'s Marty Feldman and the seminal British comedian Spike Milligan, never got off the ground. A later iteration did, via a spec script that got to Brooks through a colleague's dentist.[34] Unquestionably helpful was the renewed cultural relevance of the story thanks to Kevin Costner's mega-successful *Robin Hood: Prince of Thieves* in 1991, which trailed only *Terminator 2* in domestic box office. A few years earlier, critics had twitted *Spaceballs* for being belated, satirizing the *Star Wars* phenomenon a full decade after it had burst on the stage. No one could say the same about *Robin Hood: Men in Tights*, hitting screens twenty-five months after the Costner movie premiered.

It was, in a sense, a qualified return to form. It continued Brooks's streak of mediocre reviews, attacking the increasing creakiness and exhausted repetitiveness of his work. But over the years, it has gained its share of fans, in no small part thanks to its more audacious exploration of one of Brooks's perennial themes: Jewishness everywhere, even in the most unlikely, arguably hostile, of places. Robin of Locksley returns to England after his captivity abroad, in an opening borrowed from the Costner film, and seeks the son of his fellow prisoner, Asneeze. The odd name is a bit of a creaky set up to name the son Ahchoo, the beginning of a creaky running joke: "God bless you!" someone says, whenever his name is mentioned. But on returning to England, when the straight line is duly uttered, the first response is not the usual punchline, but: "A Jew, here?"

Yes and no: Ahchoo himself is not Jewish, but Black, played by a twenty-year-old Dave Chappelle, in an inclusive partnership of minorities by Brooks that dates back two decades. (Which is explicitly name-checked in the movie: at the film's end, he becomes sheriff of Nottingham, er, Rottingham, and when the idea is challenged, Chappelle says, "What? It worked in *Blazing Saddles!*") But there are Jews and Jewishness everywhere else in the movie.

The worst-disguised Jew in the movie is Prince John, the picture's ostensible antagonist, a villain analogous to the one Alan Rickman memorably played in *Prince of Thieves*. It may be enough to say that the role here is assayed by Richard Lewis; for those not familiar with that hand-to-head, hypochondriacal, neurasthenic comic whose viewpoint on life is adequately illustrated by the fact that he has plausibly claimed to invent the phrase "from hell," a few stray moments from the movie are worth recalling. Faced with a suckling pig, his immediate response is to yelp, "*Treyf!*" (that is, "unkosher"); presented with something more objectively unappetizing, his throwaway line ("It looks like a seder at Vincent Price's house") combines Jewishness and showbiz insiderdom with Vegas delivery. It's Jewish parody at its most basic, conflating minimization and domestication in order to control the threat—dressing down the fearful Gentile authority by presenting him as a timid, fearful Jew. (Which implies, not coincidentally, that the joke turns on the Jew, too.)

But there's a far less disguised Jew in the movie: Brooks himself, playing the movie's Judaized version of Friar Tuck, Rabbi Tuckman. Tuckman—befitting Brooks's standard conception of traditional, rabbinical Judaism as what you'd see through a contemporary American Jewish lens—is dressed anachronistically, unlike everyone else in the film, in contemporary Hasidic garb. (Although it's a *little* bit of a disguise: when the rabbi tips his hat to the Merry Men, his sidecurls come with it.)

Tuckman can express Brooks's Jewish satirical sensibility within the movie itself. His passage blocked by the Men, his response when they announce themselves is to make a hand gesture and say, skeptically, *"Feygeles?"* (Either the Yiddish or the gesture is understood by Cary Elwes's Robin, who responds, "No, no . . . we're straight. Just . . . merry.") Once again, though, Brooks burrows at the roots of the American masculine ideal, suggesting that men who dress in leggings and use Christmas-themed adjectives to describe themselves may not be the exemplars of heterosexuality that mass culture puts them forward to be, locating campiness at the heart of the American genre experience. "Let's face it," one of the Merry Men says in another scene, struggling with his hose. "You gotta be a man to wear tights!" (Then he and his compatriots burst into song, complete with can-can kickline: "We're men—MANLY MEN!—in tights . . . We're butch!")

Tuckman, another in Brooks's long line of *hondlers*, merchandises sacramental wine and expostulates on the benefits of the circumcisions he offers. ("It's the latest rage . . . the ladies love it!") When he explains, using a guillotine, the Men demur, and he muses, "I gotta work with a much younger crowd." After an offer of sacramental wine, though, the viewer is treated to shouts of "Let's hear it for the rabbi!"—presumably a rare statement offered in the actual medieval England. (It would have to have been; the Jews were expelled from the land in 1290.) But Tuckman comes to unite, not divide. Earlier in the scene, Tuckman points out that he knew Maid Marian's parents, Lord and Lady Bagelle, before they died in a plague, and he knows they're meant for each other. "What a combination? Locksley and Bagelle. Can't miss!"

Groan-worthy, yes; but again indicative. If comedies set in the forests of England are devoted (in the words of one of their most famous titles) to the notion that all's well that ends well, that what should naturally be together now is, then Brooks's screenplay points out that the natural metaphor for such a thing—one which would have seemed incongruous, of course, to watching audiences, but by no means unnatural—was a staple of American Jewish cuisine that had become an American staple more generally. Within three years of the release of *Robin Hood: Men in Tights*, a bagel company founded by an Iowa lawyer of Norwegian stock who hadn't eaten a single one until his early twenties was operating 255 stores; Bruegger's Bagels was serving three million bagels a week and bringing in about $145 million in sales a year; analysts were estimating that bagels were a billion-dollar industry.[35] Brooks, bagels, and benevolence: the enfant terrible turned kindly paterfamilias to a younger, largely Gentile cohort, just as American Jewish culture, not least food culture, was increasingly an untroubled, expansive part of the American landscape.

Brooks's role as Rabbi Tuckman, juicy as it may have been, only occupied brief snatches of screen time. He was in his late sixties by then, and the rigors of multiple roles would wear on even someone as energetic as he; plus the movie was, of course, structured around a younger action hero. And the manic, zany torch of Jewish parody had been passing to a new generation. In 1977, Gene Siskel had written that "save for the annual doses of Mel Brooks and Woody Allen, the state of film comedy is so bankrupt that movies like 'Tunnelvision' and now, 'The Kentucky Fried Movie' manage to find a considerable, mostly teenage audience."[36] But Siskel's dismissal of the two anthologies out of hand passed up the opportunity to connect their parodic, anthological sensibilities to the work of one of those currently reigning filmmaking icons. Although 1976's *Tunnel Vision* (as it's usually called) is probably most notable for the appearances of a number of *Saturday Night Live*–affiliated figures in the first bloom of their success—including Chevy Chase, Laraine Newman, Al Franken, and Tom Davis—its focus on television fit the creative influences of its Boomer creators, raised on the milieu that Brooks helped to shape.

Kentucky Fried Movie, on the other hand, was, befitting its name, more focused on parodying film genres.[37] While focusing on genres Brooks hadn't turned his attention to—including kung-fu and classroom educational films—and the filmgoing experience itself (one movie is shown in Feel-A-Round), and going places the Woodstock Generation was more comfortable with than the Greatest Generation—there is significant nudity, for example—the Jewish creative team, John Landis and the writing trio of Jim Abrahams and David and Jerry Zucker, had clearly been inspired by the constant barrage of visual and verbal gags that Brooks had brought to the screen that decade.

Landis would go on to work with other *SNL* talent in *Animal House*, the movie that took on a milieu that felt deeply goyish—the early 1960s college fraternity scene—infused it with vulgarity and, synonymously, John Belushi, and made a fortune and a career. Zucker Abrahams Zucker would turn even more explicitly to the Brooks playbook, first taking on a genre that Brooks himself had never gone after, the disaster movie. In 1980, *Airplane!*, which made approximately five times what

History of the World, Part I did for approximately one-third the budget, had the kind of gags that would have felt at home in *Young Frankenstein*—the pilot's drinking problem, for example, that consists of him being unable to direct water to his mouth, simply throwing it in his own face. But it also adopted the taut and suspenseful structure of its templates, creating genuine suspense and romantic (melo)drama nestled alongside the appearances by Lloyd Bridges and Kareem Abdul-Jabbar.[38] And, of course, it showcased the grave absurdity of Leslie Nielsen, who went on to anchor the Zucker brothers' other great parodies—the mock-police procedurals *The Naked Gun* and its two sequels, released between 1988 and 1994.

Brooks, smarting at the charges of vulgarity about *History of the World*, and by implication its box-office failure, sniffed: "I prefer to call them Rabelaisian. Look, I could have taken the easy way. I enjoyed *Airplane!* I laughed my sides out. But it didn't *dare* much. . . . [*History*] is about the eternal verities seen through the warped prism of my own observation."[39] But the audiences had spoken and they very much did not want Rabelaisian auteurism; they wanted MTV-inspired comedy with quicker cuts and video-like montages. By the mid-'90s, Brooks had resorted to relying on some of his successors' stardust, casting Leslie Nielsen in *Dracula: Dead and Loving It* (1995), about which, as a matter of mercy, we shall pass over in almost complete silence. The same goes for Brooks's TV sitcom *The Nutt House* in 1989, notable only for featuring favorite repertory players Cloris Leachman and Harvey Korman and for the rapidity of its cancellation: it lasted slightly over a month on NBC. ("The gags just didn't seem to work, even though they looked as if they should be funny," one critic wrote, which seemed to stand in for many people's sentiments about much of Brooks's most recent work.)[40]

The Zucker brothers were, in many senses, Brooks's natural successors; and, for our purposes, they also serve as a metaphor for third-generation American Jewishness. Yes, they sometimes put coded Jewish messages into their movies. In *Top Secret!*, their parody of Elvis movies and war movies—the film mashup it seems that the veteran and music-lover Brooks should absolutely have made—a waiter, ostensibly speaking German, works in a series of Yiddish lines worthy of the in-jokes in *Your Show of Shows.* But generally speaking, the Zuckers' movies were ethnically neutral: Priscilla Presley had replaced Madeline Kahn, and Leslie Nielsen—even romping around in a gigantic condom—is a lot more Dean Martin than Jerry Lewis, or Mel Brooks. Was traditional Jewish comedy essential to where Landis and the Zucker brothers had come from? Absolutely. But was it where they were going? Not necessarily.

And Brooks had, it seemed, hit a wall going forward: audience members had spoken, and it seemed like they weren't in the market for new Mel Brooks.

So the only possibility left for a man who still wanted to work, who wanted to find an audience, was to give them Old Mel Brooks. All over again.

————◆❙◆❙◆————

Epilogue

A YEAR AFTER the debacle that was *Dracula: Dead and Loving It*, Mel Brooks began his comeback. And although he hadn't gotten small, not in the least, the pictures and screens he appeared on had.

During most of Brooks's film career, there was real discomfiture with the presentation of Jewish figures on television. The one that probably stung the most for older audiences was *Bridget Loves Bernie*, the highest-rated network show ever to be cancelled—it had placed fifth in the ratings in 1972. The cancellation was ostensibly the result of popular objection, but, given the ratings, the objection couldn't have been *too* popular; it probably had a lot more to do with Jewish television executives' concerns about seeming too Jewish on television. Audiences a generation younger—or, probably more likely, the same audiences a generation older—would have bemoaned the disappearance of Jackie Mason's sitcom *Chicken Soup*, which in 1989 became the *second* highest-rated network show ever to be cancelled, for apparently similar reasons.

But the early 1990s saw a revolution in the presentation of Jews, and comedians, on television. Or, perhaps better put, a cyclical return; much like in the 1950s, a wide variety of stage performers were getting their own shows: but less from the variety stages and more from the stand-up circuit, in shows that were modeled on some mélange of their stand-up acts and their autobiography. First among equals, of course, was *Seinfeld*, which paved the way for the widespread presentation of Jews on primetime television—as long as their Jewishness was fairly bland and unobtrusive. Seinfeld's "Jerry Seinfeld" fit that bill, as did his compatriot on NBC's must-see TV, Ross Geller on *Friends*, played by David Schwimmer.

But whereas Seinfeld's show would go on to become spikier and more metaphorically (though not very explicitly) Jewish over the years—thanks, in no small part, to the collaboration with Larry David—a third character echoed Geller in remaining ethnically neutral: *Mad About You*'s Paul Buchman, played by Paul Reiser. *Mad About You*, like *Bridget Loves Bernie* a show about an intermarried couple, was, unlike it, not a show about intermarriage. It was a show, as so many sitcoms premiering in the wake of *Seinfeld* were, about nothing; early episodes revolve around things like sofa-shopping and doing the *New York Times* crossword puzzle. But Reiser's character, like Reiser the individual and Reiser the stand-up comedian, was Jewish; and so Jewishness entered. But generationally. And this is where Brooks came in.

Brooks had appeared briefly on *The Tracey Ullman Show* in 1990, playing a sleazy producer (he later returned the favor by casting her as Latrine in *Robin Hood: Men in Tights*), but his television appearances in recent years had been largely limited to guest appearances on talk shows. On *Mad About You*, though, Brooks appeared as Paul Buchman's Uncle Phil, making four appearances between 1996 and 1999 and winning Emmys for three of them. Reiser had written the role explicitly for Brooks because he was such a fan of the 2,000-Year-Old Man.[1] In all his appearances, Brooks channels the character, but, even more, the Mel Brooks his fans had grown to know over the decades in a slightly softer, more nostalgic and lovable key: wild (at least when it came to his windswept hair), obstreperous (but *family*), walking the line between hinged and un-.[2]

It wasn't just stunt casting; it wasn't just getting an excellent performer to provide a jolt of comic energy to the show, although it was both of those things, too. It was providing a very different *kind* of comic energy, and providing a genealogy both comic and Jewish. And so, a lion in winter, Brooks would continue to return back to older ground, appealing to an aging audience, serving—as the record showed—more as a symbol of an old-time Jewishness that had passed for many rather than what currently was. In 1996, the first year Brooks played the role, he participated in a very well-received reunion of the Caesar writers on PBS.[3] In 1998, the same year he won his second Emmy in a row for playing Uncle Phil—thirty years after he first won one—Brooks also won his first Grammy, forty-seven years after his first nomination. It was with Carl Reiner, the same partner from that first time, for the same characters, for the album *The 2,000-Year-Old Man in the Year 2000*. And, at the urging of David Geffen ("He was like a terrier," Brooks said; "I couldn't shake him off"), he'd partnered with an old colleague, Thomas Meehan, who'd worked on *To Be or Not to Be* and *Spaceballs*, the arranger Glen Kelly, and the white-hot choreographer Susan Stroman—whose *Contact*, a dance show with a rock and roll sensibility, had turned heads at Lincoln Center—to restage *The Producers* as a Broadway musical.[4]

Brooks, as we've seen, had always been a frustrated suitor of Broadway, and had dramatized that frustration in the original *Producers*, a movie about the theater, a statement at one remove, about people who can only achieve theatrical success by accident and malfeasance. *The Producers* the musical, then, was in many ways a revenge on his fictional and actual background: or, at least, that was how it turned out. Many of Brooks's interviews around the premiere of the musical are fraught with diffidence, in a way that shifts between faux-modest and actually humble, about his taking on the music and lyric-writing task himself.

It worked out. *The Producers* the musical triumphed on Broadway. It set a new standard for commercial and critical success, winning twelve Tonys out of fifteen nominations, a record. (*Hamilton*, in many senses the next-generation equivalent to *The Producers*, did earn more nominations, but ended up winning one fewer; and besides, winning all fifteen would have been mathematically impossible, as some nominees were competing against each other in the acting categories.) Brooks himself won three of those Tonys, for best musical, book, and score; he thanked Hitler, among others. This also elevated him, if one keeps this kind of score—and Brooks certainly did—to one of the extraordinarily small number of EGOT winners who have won, in competitive rather than honorary categories, an Emmy, a Grammy, an Oscar, and a Tony. (Brooks and Mike Nichols both achieved the milestone in the same year, 2001, the eighth and ninth people to do so.)

The Producers was also a commercial milestone for both Brooks and Broadway theater. It was the first hundred-dollar ticket on Broadway, with specially designated seats going for almost five times that much during the heat of the run.[5] And Brooks was indeed a producer of the show, and the Broadway version alone ran for 2,502 performances over six years and sold $300 million worth of tickets; by 2009, the show had grossed more than a billion dollars worldwide. It even appeared in Berlin at the Admiralspalast theater, where Adolf Hitler had gone to watch operetta.[6]

Ben Brantley wrote in the *New York Times* that "for a production that makes a point of being tasteless, *The Producers* exudes a refreshing air of innocence," and felt "defanged . . . biting the hand that feeds him, but at the same time he is kissing it quite sincerely." *The New York Review of Books* went even further, saying that the musical version "risks absolutely nothing; there's nothing at stake any more. Brooks's new musical has smoothly processed his movie, whose greatest virtue was its anarchic, grotesque energy, into a wholly safe evening."[7] If the stage success of *The Producers* was in no small part about the acceptance of Mel Brooks as a mainstream figure, domesticated and ensconced in the bosom of American entertainment, and America, it also suggested the acceptance of an unabashed and unapologetic Jewishness at the central nexus of American popular entertainment.[8] Brooks had crashed and burned on Broadway with *All-American;* and now he thrived, in the cultural world he had helped shape, *as* All-American: because that was what *The Producers*, in its film release marginal and on the edges, had become. In 2001, there was no way that the show *The Producers* could be seen as anything but mainstream itself. "A decade or two or three after his greatest triumphs on film, he's cool all over again. He's got heat," a *Boston Globe* profile cooed.[9]

Brooks himself would sometimes forget or fail to come to terms with the scope of this achievement, of the shadow he had cast on the landscape. Some of it, admittedly, was for other parts of his legacy. There was some debate, for example, over whether to put in the word "fuck" in the song "The King of Broadway," as in, "Who do you have to fuck to get a break in this town?" Concerned when it got gasps at a Pittsburgh tryout, Brooks and Meehan changed it to "shtupp." When the star Nathan Lane, who was playing Bialystock, objected, Brooks told him: "You can't say fuck in a musical!" Lane's response: "Have we met? *You're Mel Brooks!*" The word was restored.[10] In these later years, Carl Reiner and Mel Brooks—Old Men of the 2000s, one might say—would spend evenings together, sitting back and watching TV movies and doing crosswords. One time, according to Reiner, they had a discussion after a sketch on *Saturday Night Live* that revolved around farting. "I said, 'Mel, you have opened up farts to the world of entertainment,'" Reiner recalled. "'Ever since the campfire scene, everyone's using farts.' Mel sometimes doesn't like dirty jokes on television. But I said, 'Mel, you started it!'"[11]

But there was the other legacy as well. It was, without a doubt, *The Producers* that was in Mike Nichols's mind, commercially and aesthetically, when he helped launch another adapted movie on the Broadway stage just four years later. Eric Idle's *Spamalot*, the Broadway version of *Monty Python and the Holy Grail*, became perhaps best known for its second-act patter song, in which it diagnosed, tongue in cheekily but not really, the reasons it might fail to replicate the monster success of *The Producers*. The plot requires King Arthur to stage a musical on Broadway—it's just that, in the words of the song's title, "you won't succeed on Broadway/If you don't have any Jews." This leads to *Fiddler* parodies from the stage and knowing laughs from the audience: look, the funniest Gentiles in the history of popular entertainment know—and bow to—the real score. It was one thing for Brooks to plop Rabbi Tuckman into his Sherwood Forest: but the Pythons channeling Tevye . . .

And there was certainly yet an additional triumphalism, especially as *The Producers* was written and produced in the months before 9/11: that Brooks's form of anti-anti-Semitism had triumphed. The Nazis had become a total punchline, and not a barbed one, but a silly, showbizzy one at that. "Congratulations. *Hitler* will run forever," reads the telegram that Bialystock and Bloom receive at the end of the movie, and for the last years of the twentieth century and the first years of the twenty-first, *The Producers*, in both its iterations, cleared the way for the "Nazi"-fication of humor—that is, the throwing around of the term, ranging from *Seinfeld's* "Soup Nazi" to *Difficult People's* Nazi memorabilia collector and thus unsuitable boyfriend. Audiences looking at the kickline weren't thinking about Nazis, but about their memories of the filmed version of that kickline: feeling safe in their seats at the St. James Theatre. Feeling at home.

Things, alas, change. It's probably coincidental that it was almost exactly at the same time *The Producers* bowed on Broadway that Mike Godwin created his famous law stating that in on-line discussions the probability of calling someone a Nazi approached one; what was less coincidental was the way the last two decades have seen the Internet facilitate the rise of new support for Nazism and for white supremacy in ways largely unimaginable in 2001, and even in 1968. (Brooks, who'd always looked to the past, was never, and has never been, much of an Internet guy; his best friend and partner Carl Reiner, by contrast, made quite a presence for himself in the Twitterverse before his death in 2020.) And after the horrific displays of neo-Nazi activity online and in places like Charlottesville in recent years, it is fairly clear that the treatment of Nazism is going to require some rethinking in comedy.

Take, for example, the case of Larry David, one of Brooks's most significant comic descendants. Coming into his own decades after Brooks paved the way and with the benefits of a very different medium (not TV, HBO), David was able to make a meal of material Brooks was able to touch on in his movies, but still only glancingly. If Brooks could poke fun at Jesus in *History of the World*, a generation later David was able to literally piss on a picture of the Savior and—some angry letters aside—get away with it completely. But David is all about showing his comedic debts—he casts Shelley Berman as his father, for example—and his relationship to Brooks was most obviously apparent in the 2003 season of his HBO show *Curb Your Enthusiasm*, whose season-long arc revolves around Brooks casting Larry David as

Max Bialystock in the L.A. regional production of *The Producers*. The meta-joke within the show, of course, is that "Brooks" is pulling the precise scheme of *The Producers:* he knows Larry is totally unqualified and will destroy the show, thus putting all this *Producers*-mania to an end. Of course, things end badly, which is to say, well: somehow, the woeful Larry triumphs in the role, which dismays a watching Brooks and Bancroft. Brooks enjoyed the scheme tremendously, and was deeply grateful to David for providing him the opportunity to perform with Bancroft one final time before her death from cancer in 2005.[12]

But there are differences between the two iconic Jewish comedians. Asked in 2001, "You've made fun of Hitler. Is there somewhere comedy cannot go?" Brooks replied: "Yeah, a little further into Jewish concentration camps. It's just simply too heartbreaking to try to have fun with. You can't go there." Always an entertainer, a pleaser, he adds, "But you can go to any Chinese restaurant."[13] The topper falls flat, though, because of course there is no topper. In 2017, David, hosting *Saturday Night Live*, did indeed go there, or tried to, offering in his opening monologue a joke about chatting up women in a concentration camp. It flopped. On the other hand, a few years earlier, in *Curb Your Enthusiasm*, David had come up with what may still be one of the great examples of comedy about the Holocaust—juxtaposing a survivor of the camps, through absurd circumstance, with an alumnus of the TV reality show *Survivor*, whose inability to see the incomparability of their two experiences is itself a scathing satire of the same inclination the Internet has to call everything Nazism and Holocaust.[14]

Brooks has other heirs as well. His championing of bodily functions and general vulgarity has found its match—its superior—on *Broad City* in the work of Abbi Jacobson and Ilana Glazer, perhaps the most fearless comedians of the body working in recent years. Like Brooks, much of their art stems from their commitment to putting things on the screen that generally aren't there—in their case, primarily, millennial women's perspectives, replete with Madeline Kahn's sexuality but far more explicit. The complications of identity mean that for them, like for Brooks, these treatments are largely inseparable from their Jewishness: whether in an episode like "Knockoffs" where subpar sexual aids are discussed at a shiva, or trying to find tampons on a Birthright Israel flight to the Holy Land. Are these stories Brooks could have told, or even would have? Hard to imagine. Are they able to be told because of the trails he blazed, heirs of farting cowboys and pee-pee-talking psychoanalysts and French Revolution–era piss boys? Unquestionably. Only more so.

Brooks would step back substantially after Bancroft's death from cancer in 2005, spending many of his evenings having dinner, watching *Jeopardy*, and screening movies with Carl Reiner at Reiner's house (in the early months of the coronavirus pandemic, before Reiner's death, they called each other to watch the game shows socially distanced).[15] Commercially speaking, the failure of his *Producers* follow-up, a musical version of *Young Frankenstein* in 2007, curtailed the momentum in that nostalgic direction. Brooks stood to make almost a quarter of the show's profits after investors were paid back ("After *Shinbone Alley*, stay with me, after *All American* starring Ray Bolger, after four or five Broadway shows where I worked for two or three years and didn't make a paycheck, am I not entitled to 24 percent of the show if it is a big hit?"). Trying to make it so, financially at least, premium tickets were sold for $450 a pop out of the gate—which attracted a good deal of head-shaking and hand-wringing, which Brooks blamed for the musical's failure. A typical review mixed the critical and commercial aspects: "I don't mean to say that *Young Frankenstein* elicits a shrug only because it fails to live up to its mighty antecedents. The show turns out to be longish and dullish in its own right—so much so that paying the much-buzzed-about ticket price of $450 seems at least as silly as anything on the stage."[16] One couldn't call *Young Frankenstein*, which was capitalized at a record $16 million and ran for 485 performances, a failure, precisely, but it was critically savaged in its New York incarnation. A proposed *Blazing Saddles* musical never got off the ground—perhaps, in part, due to changing perspectives not on the movie's anti-racist message, but its N-word laden method of delivery ("[Using] the N-word was tricky, and to this day it's very tricky," Brooks said in a recent interview, in a rare case of understatement).[17]

Similarly, the movie adaptation of the musical adaptation of the movie *The Producers* ("I think the only thing left is animation," Brooks said) failed to make its budget back domestically in its 2005 release, and received decidedly mixed reviews.[18] Whether coincidentally or not, it was also somewhat de-Judaized in the process, those edges—and others—sanded off in trying to appeal to a wider audience: in many ways at odds with the operating method of Brooks's career.[19] This all mattered quite deeply to Brooks, of course, for whom working, moving forward in front of an audience, was life—at the time of this writing, an actual "History of the World, Part II" series, joke no longer, is on order at Hulu—but none of that mattered to the legacy.

Brooks was feted as the revered elder statesman of American culture that he was, becoming a Kennedy Center honoree in 2009, the closest thing possible to an official bestowal of a presidential seal of approval on a performing artist. "I agree 100 percent," Brooks said about the decision. "I am a national treasure. I should be celebrated. And I hope against hope that you won't find my award on eBay, because you never know."[20] (Presenting him with the award, President Obama also quoted Brooks's famous line to the effect that, in looking at Jewish history, "unrelieved lamenting would be intolerable; so every ten Jews, God designed one to be crazy and amuse the others—and by the time I was five I knew I was that one.")[21] It was followed by an American Film Institute life achievement award in 2013, a spot on the Hollywood Walk of Fame in 2014 (in which Brooks colluded with *The Walking Dead*'s makeup department to provide him with a prosthetic sixth finger for his left handprint), and a National Medal of Arts and Humanities presented by President Obama in 2016. The United States Marine Band played "Springtime for Hitler"; Brooks mock-buckled when the medal was put around his neck by President Obama, who said, echoing Brooks's joke from seven years earlier, "We'll catch you if you sell it on eBay."[22] That same year, the Writers Guild voted on the 101 funniest screenplays. Brooks had written or co-written two out of the top ten, and three in the top twelve—*Young Frankenstein* at number 6, *Blazing Saddles* at 8, and *The Producers* at 12.

Summing up that legacy, though, is something mighty: it requires thinking about the entire legacy of Jewish comedy, and, in many ways, nothing less than the Jewish encounter with America. Brooks is necessarily, foundationally, *provably* part of that story. But what lessons are to be drawn from his undeniable and magnificent successes is, of course, a different question.

In a famous, novella-length *New Yorker* profile of Brooks in 1978, the English critic Kenneth Tynan wrote, somewhat snidely and barbedly:

> I take my leave. Brooks clicks heels and bows, saying, "Your obedient Jew." He misses no opportunity to brandish his Jewishness, which he uses less as a weapon than a shield. Remember (he seems to be pleading) that I must be liked, because it is nowadays forbidden to dislike a Jew.[23]

Tynan's old school–tie anti-Semitism is showing a bit here; and, incisive critic that he was on Brooks and on much else, he seems to have missed the point in part. Brooks certainly pleaded to be liked, on many an occasion, and certainly used his sense of humor for the purpose; but he hardly would have relied on a proclamation of his Jewishness to do so. Jewishness a *shield* for

Brooks? A *means* of being liked? Unimaginable. "Your obedient Jew" was a snarling challenge, irony-saturated; remember that this was one of the most successful directors in Hollywood at the time, steeped in show-business hierarchies no less meaningful than the English social class system Tynan had made his career navigating. And Brooks was never, ever, obedient. Even when he was worshipful.

But Tynan was right, of course, that Brooks's Jewishness wasn't a weapon, either, not exactly. Because Brooks never wielded it that way. Except, and depending on your perspective this might be quite a caveat, as it infused his scalpel-sharp satire and his deadly parody. In that sense it was both arms and armor. Jewishness provided the roots of Brooks's comedy, and it protected him from the disillusionments of that comedy's failure to take hold, especially at the beginning. It helped him to look backward, for his source material and otherwise, and to look forward, to stardom and artistic success—just as historical longing and utopian optimism have always been the stalwart poles of not just Jewish comedy, but Jewish identity. The earliest book of Jewish literature, the Hebrew Bible, focuses on times before its composition (or revelation, if you prefer); and messianic redemption is always a possibility. And that tension is where Brooks—and Jews—always seem to live.

There's a joke that seems to fit, here at the end. It's a joke that's set in the shtetl, where a stranger comes to visit the small town, and, at the outskirts, sees a man sitting in a chair, looking out into the middle distance.

"What are you doing?" the stranger asks, confused.

"Ah, well. You see, I'm here to watch the graveyard. When the messiah comes, and blows his mighty ram's horn, the dead will rise from their graves and come to meet their families before heading to the Holy Land. It's my job to watch for them, and then, before they arrive, to run and tell the community that the messiah has indeed arrived and the Redemption is at hand."

"I see!" the stranger said. "An important job. How much are you paid for doing it?"

"Five kopecks a day," responded the watcher.

The stranger frowned. "That seems like rather a low sum."

"It is," the watcher said. "But, you know, it's steady work."

A traditional joke with decidedly uncomfortable corollaries: one both deeply at home with its Jewishness and rambunctious about its implications. But it exists, safe in the bosom of Jewish humor, because it shines with love and affection for the community it mocks. Brooks was disobedient, yes. But he was also always ours: as Jews, as Americans, as audience. He wore his kishkes on his sleeve, and he won the hearts that were on ours.

Introduction

1. Maurice Yacowar, *Method in Madness: The Comic Art of Mel Brooks* (St. Martin's, 1981), 10.

Chapter 1. A Jew Grows in Brooklyn

1. Abraham Raisin, "His Trip to America," in *The New Country*, ed. Henry Goodman (Syracuse University Press, 2001), 39–42.
2. See Patrick McGilligan, *Funny Man: Mel Brooks* (Harper-Collins, 2019), 1–19; the quotation is from Brad Darrach, "Mel Brooks: The Playboy Interview," *Playboy*, February 1975.
3. In Marc Eliot, *Song of Brooklyn: An Oral History of America's Favorite Borough* (New York: Broadway, 2008), 131, 129. See also Will Holtzman, *Seesaw: A Dual Biography of Anne Bancroft and Mel Brooks* (Doubleday, 1979), 4.
4. Lynda Gorov, "Mel Brooks, King of the Politically Incorrect," *Moment Magazine*, October 11, 2011; James Robert Parish,

It's Good to Be the King: The Seriously Funny Life of Mel Brooks (John Wiley, 2007), 15.

5. Rose Eichenbaum, *The Director Within* (Wesleyan University Press, 2014), 158.

6. Brooks, "Springtime for the Music Man in Me," *New York Times*, April 15, 2001. Brooks fondly remembers his mother's singing, suspecting his love of music is inherited from her; see Mel Brooks, *All About Me! My Remarkable Life in Show Business* (Ballantine, 2021), 8.

7. Quoted in McGilligan, *Funny Man*, 10.

8. Roger Ebert, "Brooks Back in the Saddle Again," *Los Angeles Times*, November 15, 1977. He presumably saw it on re-release: it was originally released in New York in 1928.

9. "Some dump": in McGilligan, *Funny Man*, 17; compare Holtzman, *Seesaw*, 6. See also Robert Weide, "Quiet on the Set!" *DGA Quarterly*, Summer 2012, and Kam Williams, "Mel Brooks Makes a Noise," *Philadelphia Sunday Sun*, May 17, 2013; Brooks, *All About Me!* 34–36.

10. Eliot, *Song of Brooklyn*, 132.

11. Darrach, "Playboy Interview"; McGilligan, *Funny Man*, 14; Brooks, *All About Me!* 28–31, quote 30.

12. McGilligan, *Funny Man*, 26–30; Joyce Haber, "N.Y. Showman Mel Brooks Arrives in Hollywood," *Los Angeles Times*, November 1, 1970; Margo Whitmire, "Q&A: Mel Brooks," *Hollywood Reporter*, December 8, 2005; Parish, *It's Good to Be the King*, 32–33; Brooks, *All About Me!* 32–33.

13. Darrach, "Playboy Interview"; Brooks, *All About Me!* 39–40.

14. Yacowar, *Method in Madness*, 16.

15. Kenneth Tynan, "Frolics and Detours of a Short Hebrew Man," *New Yorker*, October 30, 1978, 78.

16. Compare Holtzman, *Seesaw*, 10–11.

17. Joanne Stang, "And Then He Got Smart," *New York Times*, January 30, 1966.

18. McGilligan, *Funny Man*, 34–35; Brooks, *All About Me!* 47–48.

19. Mel Brooks, "Williamsburg Days," in *Brooklyn: A State of Mind*, ed. Michael W. Robbins (Workman: 2000), 117.

20. Gorov, "Mel Brooks."

21. Tynan, "Frolics," 80.

22. Parish, *It's Good to Be the King*, 47.

23. McGilligan, *Funny Man*, 42–43; Brooks, *All About Me!* 70.

24. He'd also been the social director at Butler Lodge in summer 1946. McGilligan, *Funny Man*, 45–51; Holtzman, *Seesaw*, 28–32.

25. Bosley Crowther, "'Copacabana,' Film That Tells of Night-Club Shenanigans, Is New Bill at the Broadway—Groucho Marx Chief Interest," *New York Times*, July 12, 1947.

26. Tynan, "Frolics," 82.

27. See McGilligan, *Funny Man*, 54–55, and Holtzman, *Seesaw*, 34–37, 52–55.

28. See Burt Prelutsky, "'Show': Lazarus of Kines," *Los Angeles Times*, April 22, 1973. Brooks describes his first punch-up of a sketch for Caesar, while he was still on *The Admiral Broadway Revue*, as one where Caesar plays a "jungle boy" in the city, who fears fighting only one thing: a Buick. Darrach, "Playboy Interview." For Caesar's perspective on the show, see, for example, his *Where Have I Been?: An Autobiography* (Crown, 1982), esp. 91–106.

29. Maurice Zolotow, "Treasure Chest or Idiot Box?" *Cosmopolitan*, December 1957, 33.

30. Parish, *It's Good to Be the King*, 84.

31. Holtzman, *Seesaw*, 91; Brooks, *All About Me!* 90–91.

32. Yacowar, *Method in Madness*, 3–4; Tynan, "Frolics," 123; Dennis McLellan, "Mel Tolkin, 1913–2007," *Los Angeles Times*, November 27, 2007.

33. McGilligan, *Funny Man*, 69–77; Eichenbaum, *The Director Within*, 162–163.

34. Quoted in Yacowar, *Method in Madness*, 36. See, however, Brooks, *All About Me!* 98–99.

35. On *Caesar's Hour* particularly, Larry Gelbart and the Simon brothers were also specialists in the parodies; see William Grimes, "Forty Years Later, the Laughter's Still Loud," *New York Times*, August 18, 1996.

36. Goodman Ace, *The Book of Little Knowledge: More Than You Want to Know About Television* (New York: Simon and Schuster, 1955), 153; McGilligan, *Funny Man*, 97.

37. "It's a Baby Boy for the Caesars," *Boston Sunday Globe*, February 24, 1952.

38. "Chatter: Miami Beach," *Variety*, March 12, 1952.

39. Ace, *Book*.

40. *Variety*, January 7, 1953, 108–113.

41. Sam Zolotow, "'Curtain Going Up' to Arrive Feb. 28," *New York Times*, January 2, 1952.

42. "100G Budget on 'Curtain' Revue," *Variety*, January 9, 1952.

43. Parish, *It's Good to Be the King*, 16; Brooks, *All About Me!* 17–20.

44. "Plays Out of Town," *Variety*, February 20, 1952.

45. On whose staff was Sheldon Harnick, who went on to write the lyrics for *Fiddler on the Roof;* see McGilligan, *Funny Man*, 86–87.

46. For a measured treatment, see Samuel G. Freedman, "Since the Opening Curtain, a Question: Is Willy Loman Jewish?" *New York Times*, May 18, 2012.

47. *Variety*, June 4, 1952.

48. See Holtzman, *Seesaw*, 96–97.

49. See Carl Reiner, *My Anecdotal Life* (St. Martin's Press, 2003), 52–54; Parish, *It's Good to Be the King*, 72.

50. Tynan, "Frolics," 92–93.

51. Quoted in Holtzman, *Seesaw*, 166.

52. Reiner, *My Anecdotal Life*, 56–57.

53. McGilligan, *Funny Man*, 98, 101.

54. "Tele Follow-Up Comment," *Variety*, January 14, 1953.

55. He'd previously briefly worked on a different Rita Hayworth picture, *Pal Joey;* on this earlier experience, see Brooks's recollections in *All About Me!* 105–108.

56. "Television Reviews," *Variety*, September 16, 1953.

57. Sam Zolotow, "Beaumont Ends Guild-Wilson Tie," *New York Times*, July 12, 1954.

58. McGilligan, *Funny Man*, 115.

NOTES TO PAGES 30–37

59. "'The Vamp' Begins Its Run Tonight," *New York Times*, November 10, 1955.

60. "Some Early Portents," *Variety*, October 6, 1954; compare McGilligan, *Funny Man*, 116–117. Brooks had gotten some first brief directing experience on *Your Show of Shows*, putting comedy sketches on their feet before the live show; see *All About Me!* 96.

61. McGilligan, *Funny Man*, 121; Parish, *It's Good to Be the King*, 96–97; Holtzman, *Seesaw*, 113–117.

62. Louis Calta, "New Team Formed To Produce Revue," *New York Times*, February 5, 1955; "J.V. Reed Heads Board of Shakespeare Festival," *New York Herald Tribune*, February 12, 1955; "Three Nights of Thurber," *New York Herald Tribune*, February 20, 1955.

63. "Caesar's Hour," *Variety*, September 28, 1955.

64. "TV 'Emmy' Nominees Named by DeFore; Daly Emcees Eastern Awards," *Los Angeles Times*, February 24, 1956.

65. See Holtzman, *Seesaw*, 123–124; compare different accounts in McGilligan, *Funny Man*, 137.

66. Zolotow, "Treasure Chest," 32.

67. See Lewis Funke, "News and Gossip of the Rialto," *New York Times*, April 14, 1957.

68. Lewis Funke, "News and Gossip of the Rialto," *New York Times*, March 10, 1957.

69. "B'Way Blitzed," *Variety*, April 10, 1957.

70. Sam Zolotow, "Summer Shows in Queens to End," *New York Times*, April 9, 1957.

71. Although, as *Variety* noted, he would keep his contractual royalty as director. "Legit Bits," *Variety*, April 10, 1957; "'Shinbone Alley' On Stage Tonight," *New York Times*, April 13, 1957.

72. Quoted in Gilbert Millstein, "A Musical Alley: French Farce and New York Musical on the Week's Schedule," *New York Times*, April 7, 1957. On the play, see Yacowar, *Method in Madness*, 22.

73. Millstein, "A Musical Alley"; "Openings of the Week," *New York Times*, April 7, 1957.

74. *New York Times*, April 15, 1957.
75. Atkinson, "Shinbone Alley," *New York Times*, April 28, 1957.
76. "Shinbone Alley," *Variety*, April 16, 1957; "On Stage," *Newsday*, April 26, 1957.
77. John Chapman, *Broadway's Best, 1957: The Complete Record of the Theatrical Year* (Doubleday, 1957), 292.
78. "Shinbone Alley," *Variety*, April 17, 1957.
79. Marie Torre, "Old Comedy Will Never Die," *New York Herald Tribune*, April 9, 1957.
80. Jack O'Brian, "Radio-TV," *Daily Defender*, October 2, 1957.
81. Sam Boal, "Pretty Polly," *Cosmopolitan*, December 1957, 53.
82. "Tele Follow-Up Comment," *Variety*, October 9, 1957.
83. Mel Brooks quoted in David Bianculli, *The Platinum Age of Television* (Doubleday, 2016), 104. On the *Mad Magazine* comparison, see Henry Jenkins, "Mel Brooks, Vulgar Modernism, and Comic Remediation," in *A Companion to Film Comedy*, ed. Andrew Horton and Joanna E. Rapf (Wiley-Blackwell, 2012), 151–171, 158–159.
84. "Mend Fences on TV Vocal Shows; New Producers," *Variety*, October 30, 1957; "Polly Bergen's Third Producer," *Variety*, December 4, 1957; "If You Can't Axe It, Fix It," *Variety*, December 11, 1957.
85. Richard F. Shepard, "Two Women's Shows Will Be Replaced," *New York Times*, January 18, 1958; "Cosmetic Firm for Caesar-Coca Show," *Billboard*, September 23, 1957.
86. "Television Reviews," *Variety*, January 29, 1958.
87. Gilbert Millstein, "TV's Comics Went Thataway," *New York Times Magazine*, February 2, 1958, 14.
88. See McGilligan, *Funny Man*, 140, 145, and passim. Kitt had also appeared in *New Faces of 1952*; see Holtzman, *Seesaw*, 84.
89. McGilligan, *Funny Man*, 163–166; Parish, *It's Good to Be the King*, 129–130.
90. "CBS Plans TV Show Portraying Life Stories of Top Americans," *Newsday*, January 7, 1959.
91. Charles Witbeck, "Ginger Is Flying High Thanks to TV Work," *Hartford Courant*, May 31, 1959; Ben Kubasik, "British Comedian David King Is Ready for Spot of American TV," *Newsday*,

NOTES TO PAGES 42–49

May 20, 1959. Barbara Delatiner, "On Television," *Newsday*, May 21, 1959.

92. McGilligan, *Funny Man*, 155. See also "Look and Listen With Donald Kirkley," *The Sun*, December 4, 1959; Barbara Delatiner, "On Television," *Newsday*, December 3, 1959; Brooks, *All About Me!* 115.

93. McGilligan, *Funny Man*, 157.

94. Tynan, "Frolics," 46. See also McGilligan, *Funny Man*, 160–162.

95. Carl Reiner and Mel Brooks, *The 2000 Year Old Man* (Warner, 1981), 41.

96. He'd made a very brief appearance a decade earlier, on the Texaco Star Theater.

97. *Open End* later changed its name to *The David Susskind Show*.

98. See McGilligan, *Funny Man*, 167–169. The program was broadcast more widely in August of that year.

Chapter 2. What Next, Cancer?

1. The play appeared on May 16, 1960, under the title "archy and mehitabel." See Barbara Delatiner, "On Television," *Newsday*, May 17, 1960; and John P. Shanley, "archy and mehitabel," *New York Times*, May 17, 1960.

2. "Japanese Actors Star in Western," *New York Times*, June 27, 1960.

3. See Shawn Levy, *King of Comedy: The Life and Art of Jerry Lewis* (New York: St. Martin's, 1996), 247–261; "Jerry Lewis Signs Helen Traubel," *Newsday*, August 8, 1960; McGilligan, *Funny Man*, 151–152, 170; Brooks, *All About Me!* 137–138.

4. Quoted in Gerald Nachman, "The 2000 Year Old Man Turns 2009," *The 2000 Year Old Man: The Complete History* (DVD Collection, 2009); Reiner, *My Anecdotal Life*, 62–63.

5. *Newsday*, December 1, 1960.

6. Al Cohn, "Mel Brooks: The Laugh Is the Answer," *Newsday*, July 21, 1974.

7. Don Page, "Viewers 'Get Smarter' with Breakthrough in Hip Satire," *Los Angeles Times*, January 28, 1966.

8. Wally George, "Court of Records," *Los Angeles Times*, November 6, 1960. On Reiner's career at the time, see "Carl Reiner Has 'Noodled' Himself to Heights of TV," *Hartford Courant*, November 12, 1961; "Success May Kill Leading TV Comedy," *Hartford Courant*, February 7, 1965.

9. Quoted in Jim Barrows, "A Look at the Records," *Hartford Courant*, November 27, 1960. See also McGilligan, *Funny Man*, 175–176.

10. Tynan, "Frolics," 48.

11. See *Seventeen* magazine, June 1961 ("Popular Record Reviews," p. 47); *Redbook* ("Music for a Gay Dinner Party," September 1961, p. 22); Holtzman, *Seesaw*, 165.

12. Parish, *It's Good to Be the King*, 119.

13. *Chicago Daily Tribune*, "Previews of Today's Network TV," February 12, 1961.

14. Thomas Lask, "Comedians' Monument—A Plastic Platter," *New York Times*, January 29, 1961.

15. For transcription of the act, I rely on Reiner and Brooks, *The 2000 Year Old Man*, 29, 9, with slight changes to indicate emphasis and pronunciation.

16. Darrach, "Playboy Interview."

17. Reiner and Brooks, *The 2000 Year Old Man*, 15, 11; Brooks, *All About Me!* 126.

18. Reiner and Brooks, *The 2000 Year Old Man*, 14.

19. Reiner and Brooks, *The 2000 Year Old Man*, 25.

20. Reiner and Brooks, *The 2000 Year Old Man*, 16.

21. For the years 1960 and 1961, the comedy Grammy was divided into two separate categories, spoken comedy and musical comedy.

22. See "Comedians Signed," *Los Angeles Times*, September 22, 1961. They appear on October 18. Cecil Smith, "The Buttondown Mind Platooned," *Los Angeles Times*, October 18, 1961.

23. Murry Frymer, "You Did What? Are You Serious?" *Newsday*, June 13, 1967.

24. This account is per Douglass K. Daniel, *Anne Bancroft: A Life* (University Press of Kentucky, 2017), 87–88. Brooks, in his

memoir, claims it was a different song, "a Gertrude Niesen favorite, 'I Wanna Get Married'"; *All About Me!* 143. However, an actual recording of the presumed telecast in question—from February 22, 1961—shows Como and Bancroft dueting on a medley of love songs—in which *neither* of these two songs appears. Perhaps the song (whichever it was; maybe she tried both) was cut in rehearsal; the thrust of the repartee surrounding the medley, however, suggests Bancroft adopting a persona closer to "Married I Can Always Get" than "I Wanna Get Married." "Perry Como & Anne Bancroft Live—Love Medley," on YouTube (www.youtube.com/watch?v=dIxO91iDcTc).

25. See Holtzman, *Seesaw*, 187–188; McGilligan, *Funny Man*, 179–185, 216–219.

26. McGilligan, *Funny Man*, 402.

27. See, variously, my *The Worlds of Sholem Aleichem* (Schocken, 2013); and Alisa Solomon, *Wonder of Wonders* (Metropolitan, 2013).

28. Compare Parish, *It's Good to Be the King*, 161.

29. Judy Klemesrud, "Jewish-Gentile Marriages: As Number Grows, So Does Debate," *New York Times*, June 25, 1973.

30. Tynan, "Frolics," 105.

31. "Religious Drama Will Open Feb. 17," *New York Times*, January 20, 1961. See also Parish, *It's Good to Be the King*, 142–148.

32. See Robert Lewis Taylor, *Professor Fodorski* (Doubleday, 1950), 12, 199.

33. "'Birdie' and 'Irma' Next at Ford's," *The Sun*, January 28, 1962.

34. Quoted in Yacowar, *Method in Madness*, 65.

35. See Philip K. Scheuer, "Dorothy Lamour's 'Road' Role Builds," *Los Angeles Times*, September 19, 1961.

36. See Ken Mandelbaum, *Not Since Carrie: Forty Years of American Musical Flops* (Macmillan, 1991), 55–56, quote 56.

37. "Preston to Star as Pancho Villa," *New York Times*, September 19, 1961.

38. McGilligan, *Funny Man*, 189.

39. Sam Zolotow, "Bolger to Star in 'All American,'" *New York Times*, November 8, 1961.

40. "'All American' Shifts," *New York Times*, November 20, 1961.

41. Mandelbaum, *Not Since Carrie*, 56.

42. Review quotes from McGilligan, *Funny Man*, 194–195.

43. "Capitol Records to Issue Album as Partner of Richard Rodgers," *New York Times*, December 27, 1961.

44. "News of the Rialto," *New York Times*, December 31, 1961.

45. Lewis Lapham, "Anatomy of a Musical," *London Life*, December 4, 1965, 44.

46. Lapham, "Anatomy," 45.

47. Mandelbaum, *Not Since Carrie*, 80; McGilligan, *Funny Man*, 199–200; Lisa Rosen, "Where Did He Go Right?" *Written By*, January 2016, 39.

48. McGilligan, *Funny Man*, 197–210, quote 197; Tynan, "Frolics," 101–102.

49. Geraldine Fabrikant, "A Funny Man Earns It the 2,000 Year Old Way," *New York Times*, October 26, 1997.

50. Michael Wall, "Miss Italiano," *The Guardian*, August 28, 1963.

51. "Insecurity Still Grips Red Buttons," *Hartford Courant*, September 6, 1963.

52. Alex Freeman, "Steve Lawrence's Star Is Rising," *Hartford Courant*, December 20, 1963.

53. Philip K. Scheuer, "'Yum Yum' Sex Fails to Deter Patronage," *Los Angeles Times*, November 28, 1963.

54. Alex Freeman, "Sinatra Proves He's a Nice Guy," *Hartford Courant*, August 17, 1964.

55. Both August 11, 1964.

56. *Mel Brooks—The Critic (1963)*, on YouTube (www.youtube.com/watch?v=PramR5oxn5o).

57. *The Violinist*, on YouTube (www.youtube.com/watch?v=wlnuyZMRLr4&app=desktop).

58. Tynan, "Frolics," 106.

59. *Critic* (January 1964), 30.

60. Cecil Smith, "Video Puts in Plug for Movies," *Los Angeles Times*, March 25, 1964.

61. "Letters," *New York Times*, April 10, 1966; Tynan, "Frolics," 104.

62. McGilligan, *Funny Man*, 214.

63. It aired on April 4, 1964.

64. McGilligan, *Funny Man*, 220; quotation from Alex Freeman, "'Virginia' May Lose Gary Clarke," *Hartford Courant*, May 6, 1964. Mike Nichols had originally been attached, but had to drop out; see Parish, *It's Good to Be the King*, 163.

65. "'Smart' Promotion Gruelling to Adams," *Hartford Courant*, June 20, 1965.

66. On this, see also Marion Purcelli, "An All Thumbs Secret Agent," *Chicago Tribune*, March 19, 1966, where Adams claims even his wife thinks he's Maxwell Smart.

67. "Smart Money," *Time*, October 15, 1965, 109.

68. Jack Gould, "TV and Radio: New Programs Reviewed," *New York Times*, September 18, 1965.

69. McGilligan, *Funny Man*, 236–237.

70. Along with work he'd previously done with Bill Dana; see "Would You Believe . . . Don Adams?" *New York Times*, September 28, 1969, and Brooks, *All About Me!* 151.

71. Robert Musel, "How to Kid the James Bond Craze—Meet Maxwell Smart," *Los Angeles Times*, August 9, 1965; McGilligan, *Funny Man*, 221–224, 229, 239; Alex Freeman, "Backstage War on 'Get Smart' Set," *Hartford Courant*, January 21, 1966. See also Tynan, "Frolics," 107.

72. Several months later, an item in the press would suggest that the constant pregnancy rumors were really upsetting Bancroft: "What bothers Anne is that she very much wants to begin a family, but it hasn't happened yet and she's just superstitious enough to think maybe the phony rumors are the reason it hasn't happened." Alex Freeman, "Trouble at the Batcave," *Hartford Courant*, October 5, 1966.

73. Dorothy Kilgallen, "Mills Family Swarms Again," *Washington Post Times Herald*, February 7, 1965; Herb Lyon, "Tower Ticker," *Chicago Tribune*, August 1, 1965; Hedda Hopper, "She Wants the Best of Two Worlds: Hollywood and Broadway," *Hartford Courant*, October 31, 1965; Doreen King, "An Incandescent Actress," *Baltimore Sun*, May 26, 1966.

74. Walter Carlson, "Advertising: From Balthazar to Ballantine," *New York Times*, December 12, 1965. This followed an appearance on *The Dick Cavett Show* in 1970, when Cavett had asked Brooks to become, then served as the interlocutor with, the 2,000-Year-Old Man: see Alex Symons, "The Prolonged Celebrity of Mel Brooks: Adapting to Survive in the Multimedia Marketplace, 1961–2004," *Celebrity Studies* 2:3 (2011), 335–352, 341.

75. Walter Carlson, "Advertising: Big Brewer Changing Caves," *New York Times*, January 26, 1966.

76. Page, "Viewers 'Get Smarter.'"

77. Gould, "TV and Radio: New Programs Reviewed," September 18, 1965; see also McGilligan, *Funny Man*, 191.

78. Darrach, "Playboy Interview."

79. Williams, "Mel Brooks Makes a Noise."

80. Alex Freeman, "Mel Brooks Pens Another Series," *Hartford Courant*, January 12, 1966.

81. Sam Kashner, "The Making of *The Producers*," *Vanity Fair*, January 2004; "'Bonnie and Clyde' to Roll," *Los Angeles Times*, August 18, 1966.

82. Tynan, "Frolics," 110.

83. Stang, "And Then He Got Smart." Olsen, who'd also worked with Brooks on *Get Smart*, would serve as a model, parodied, of the secretary in *The Producers*. See also McGilligan, *Funny Man*, 248–250; Brooks, *All About Me!* 160–161.

84. See Murry Frymer, "What's Sid Been Doing? Just Taking Life Lightly," *Newsday*, April 4, 1967.

85. Barbara Delatiner, "'Twas a Night of Nights," *Newsday*, April 6, 1967.

86. See McGilligan, *Funny Man*, 254–256.

87. See "Terence Stamp Heads 'Cow' Cast," *Los Angeles Times*, May 22, 1967; Barbara Delatiner, "Award Show Gets No Emmy," *Newsday*, June 5, 1967.

88. Mary Blume, "Zero Adds Up to a Deft Comedian," *Los Angeles Times*, March 23, 1967.

89. See Norman Mark, "Up a Notch or Two from Borscht Belt," *Los Angeles Times*, July 14, 1968.

90. Gene Siskel, "No Kidding, Mel Brooks Is a Serious Film-maker," *Chicago Tribune*, November 6, 1977; Rosen, "Where Did He Go Right?" 39; Brooks, *All About Me!* 166. In his memoir, Brooks places the time of his employment for Kutcher as 1947; see *All About Me!* 74–76.

91. McGilligan, *Funny Man*, 212–213.

92. Mark, "Up a Notch or Two."

93. Compare McGilligan, *Funny Man*, 266–267.

94. Siskel, "No Kidding."

95. On the fundraising and producing, see McGilligan, *Funny Man*, 251–252, and Kashner, "Making of *The Producers*."

96. Tynan, "Frolics," 112. Brooks, in his memoir, plausibly reports that Levine also consulted local exhibitors who indicated they would refuse to show the title *Springtime for Hitler* on their marquees; *All About Me!* 165.

97. McGilligan, *Funny Man*, 262. For Levine's objections to the kickline, see *All About Me!* 176.

98. Eichenbaum, *The Director Within*, 164.

99. "'Producers' Comics Talk It Up," *Chicago Daily Defender*, June 20, 1967; Kashner, "Making of *The Producers*."

100. Joan Barthel, "Brooks: To Lie and Sound Jolly?" *New York Times*, September 3, 1967. The profile had been commissioned for *Life* as a puff piece, but given the results, the magazine passed, and the *Times* picked it up. Holtzman, *Seesaw*, 240–241.

101. Roderick Mann, "Well, We Can't All Be Louis Jourdan," *New York Times*, November 16, 1969.

102. Richard L. Coe, "Fields, Marx, and Mostel," *Washington Post*, November 22, 1967.

103. Terry Clifford, "Mel Brooks' Lunacy Makes 'The Producers' a Funny Film," *Chicago Tribune*, July 7, 1968. McGilligan, *Funny Man*, 279–280; Kashner, "Making of *The Producers*"; Cliff Rothman, "Sellers' Choice," *Los Angeles Times*, May 30, 2001.

104. R. H. Gardner, "Comedy at Two Theaters," *Baltimore Sun*, November 29, 1967; David Sterritt, "Zero Mostel Stars in Mel Brooks's *The Producers*," *Christian Science Monitor*, August 28, 1968; McGilligan, *Funny Man*, 283–284.

105. "Screen: 'The Producers' at Fine Arts," *New York Times*, March 19, 1968.

106. "Vogue's Spotlight: Movies," *Vogue*, February 15, 1968, 46.

107. Kael, "O Pioneer!" *New Yorker*, March 23, 1968.

108. See Richard L. Coe, "The Brookses Are in Action," *Washington Post*, December 15, 1967; Parish, *It's Good to Be the King*, 177.

109. Tom Milne, "The Producers," *Monthly Film Bulletin*, January 1, 1969, 234.

110. The figure for *The Producers* on boxofficemojo.com as of summer 2020 seems incorrect; I've relied on other estimates suggesting its domestic gross on first release was under $2 million. *The Graduate*, by contrast, grossed well over $100 million.

111. Vincent Canby, "The Importance of Being Oscar," *New York Times*, April 20, 1969. Brooks would also win a Writers' Guild Award for the screenplay.

112. Lorenzo St. Dubois was played by Dick Shawn, who'd replaced Mostel in *A Funny Thing Happened on the Way to the Forum*. Leo Seligsohn, "To 'Shy' Shawn, It's All an Act," *Newsday*, September 19, 1968. See Kirsten Fermaglich, "Mel Brooks' *The Producers:* Tracing American Jewish Culture Through Comedy, 1967–2007," *American Studies* 48:4 (Winter 2007), 59–87, 63–64.

113. Compare Gary Arnold, "Brooks: Help from Brahms," *Washington Post*, November 10, 1970. Late in life, Brooks said he got the novel from a frequent dinner companion, Julie Green; see *All About Me!* 141.

114. Siskel, "No Kidding."

115. Judy Klemesrud, "Tall, Dark, and Our Next Hamlet?" *New York Times*, December 1, 1968.

116. Joyce Haber, "Moody Signs for Mel Brooks' Film," *Los Angeles Times*, March 13, 1969.

117. Yacowar, *Method in Madness*, 10.

118. See Charles Champlin, "'Twelve Chairs' Opens Run," *Los Angeles Times*, October 29, 1970; McGilligan, *Funny Man*, 298.

119. Earl Wilson, "Mitchum Carefree About Jail Days," *Hartford Courant*, January 15, 1971. Brooks gives a slightly more serious

account in his memoir: the actor he'd planned on for the role fell ill, so he stepped in; *All About Me!* 196–197.

120. Joseph Gelmis, "But Seriously, Folks, Mel Brooks Is One of the Brightest People You're Gonna Run into in Your Life. Just Ask Him," *Newsday*, January 21, 1971.

121. Stephen Whitfield, "Comic Echoes of Kafka," *European Judaism* 12:2 (Winter 1978), 40.

122. Gelmis, "But Seriously, Folks."

123. Joyce Haber, "Cary Hints at a Return to Screen," *Los Angeles Times*, November 26, 1970.

124. Quoted in Yacowar, *Method in Madness*, 88.

125. McGilligan, *Funny Man*, 302–305.

126. Philip H. Dougherty, "Advertising: A Different Banana," *New York Times*, May 24, 1972; quotation in Leonard Sloane, "Advertising: Bic Fall Campaign," *New York Times*, Aug, 10, 1973. The ads won "a pair of Clios."

127. Quoted in Parish, *It's Good to Be the King*, 191.

Chapter 3. Breaking Clichés

1. Tynan, "Frolics," 119. Brooks later supported Begelman when he was caught in a check-forging scandal: see Bill Farr, "Begelman Gets Probation, Fine in $40,000 Forgery," *Los Angeles Times*, June 29, 1978; David McClintick, "Columbia Pictures's Begelman Case Seen Ending as Bizarrely as It Began," *Wall Street Journal*, December 20, 1977.

2. McGilligan, *Funny Man*, 307–312, quote 310. Compare Brooks, *All About Me!* 206–207, on the assemblage of the writers' room.

3. Adam Pockross, "Mel Brooks on Blazing New Comedic Trails in 'Blazing Saddles,'" *Yahoo! Entertainment*, May 7, 2014.

4. It might also have been related to the fact that there was an earlier movie called *Black Bart*, starring Dan Duryea and Yvonne De Carlo, in 1948. That Bart, needless to say, was not Black. See "The Warpath," *Chicago Tribune*, November 11, 1973.

5. A. H. Weiler, "New Twist on the West," *The Sun*, November 26, 1972.

6. Russell Davies, "Laughs Out West," *The Observer*, June 23, 1974.

7. McGilligan, *Funny Man*, quotes 313, 340.

8. Yacowar, *Method in Madness*, 3; "The Warpath."

9. The phrasing appears in the Weiler article, for example.

10. Quoted in Yacowar, *Method in Madness*, 103.

11. See Tynan, "Frolics," 121–122.

12. McGilligan, *Funny Man*, 319. Compare Jenkins, "Mel Brooks, Vulgar Modernism," 161–162, and Yacowar, *Method in Madness*, 113–115.

13. Siskel, "No Kidding."

14. Tynan, "Frolics," 106.

15. Darrach, "Playboy Interview."

16. Compare Sanford Pinsker, "The Instruments of American-Jewish Humor," *Massachusetts Review* 22:4 (Winter 1981), 739–750, esp. 744–745. For a different interpretation of the Native American scene, compare Yacowar, *Method in Madness*, 110–111.

17. Brooks had actually offered him the Hedley Lamarr part that eventually went to Harvey Korman; Wilder turned it down, feeling he wasn't a good fit. And, in what would have been even odder casting, Brooks apparently offered the Young/Wilder part to Johnny Carson, and, by his own account, to John Wayne. McGilligan, *Funny Man*, 328–329; Parish, *It's Good to Be the King*, 8; Brooks, *All About Me!* 216–217.

18. "The Warpath."

19. Weide, "Quiet on the Set!"

20. Charles Champlin, "Was the West Ever Like This?" *Los Angeles Times*, February 7, 1974.

21. Jan Dawson, "Blazing Saddles," *Monthly Film Bulletin*, January 1974, 120–121.

22. See Judith Kinnard, "Brooks, Reiner Revive 2,000 Year Old Man, Now 2,013: Appreciative Audience," *New York Times*, August 27, 1973.

23. "Pop Album Briefs," *Los Angeles Times*, November 11, 1973. See also Lou Seligsohn, "Records," *Newsday*, November 13, 1973;

Loraine Alterman, "The 2,013 Year Old Man Returns," *New York Times*, November 18, 1973. The album also included very early material—from between 1954 and 1957—recorded at Fire Island, previously unreleased since it was considered too risqué at the time. "Risque Release," *Newsday*, September 16, 1973.

24. Joy Gould Boyum, "The New Vogue of 'Good Pals,'" *Wall Street Journal*, February 15, 1974.

25. Champlin, "Was the West Ever Like This?" For a particularly vicious example of the criticism of the movie, see Gary Arnold, "'Blazing Saddles' on a Dead Horse," *Washington Post*, March 7, 1974.

26. See "Mel Brooks Begs to Differ," *New York Times*, June 2, 1974.

27. Maurice Peterson, "Willie Dynamite, Blazing Saddles, and Others," *Essence*, May 1974, 16. See also Brooks, *All About Me!* 209–210.

28. Greg Nims, "Saddles Blaze in Fun Film," *Chicago Defender*, April 6, 1974.

29. Weide, "Quiet on the Set!"

30. "Hedy Lamarr Files Suit for $10 Million," *Los Angeles Times*, June 17, 1974.

31. Tynan, "Frolics," 58.

32. "Mel Brooks Plans a Horror Show," *New York Times*, August 26, 1973.

33. See "It Started Ten Feet Off Ground and Never Came Back to Earth," *Chicago Defender*, December 21, 1974, and Mc-Gilligan, *Funny Man*, 270–271, 334–335.

34. Wayne Warga, "The Birth of a Mirthful Monster," *Los Angeles Times*, April 14, 1974. The builder was Ken Strickfaden, who received the title of technical director.

35. Gerald Hirschfeld, "The Story Behind the Filming of 'Young Frankenstein,'" *American Cinematographer*, July 1974.

36. Gary Arnold, "Monstrous Spoof," *Washington Post*, December 21, 1974.

37. Tynan, "Frolics," 68. Interestingly, Brooks, in his memoir,

NOTES TO PAGES 113–118

suggests that Wilder came up with the Ritz gag, and Brooks protested its inclusion up through its overwhelming reception at a test screening; see *All About Me!* 245–247.

38. Compare Robert Kerwin's contemporary profile of Boyle, "A Nice Guy with a Zipper in His Neck," *Chicago Tribune*, June 23, 1974.

39. Charles Champlin, "Portrait of a Young Monster," *Los Angeles Times*, December 18, 1974. More autobiographically, Brooks claimed that by making Frankenstein into a "friendly guy," he was exorcising his childhood fears; Parish, *It's Good to Be the King*, 27.

40. Cohn, "Mel Brooks."

41. Compare Madeline Kahn's comments on Brooks's female characters in Bart Mills, "Mel's Clown Princess," *The Guardian*, October 8, 1981.

42. Vincent Canby, "'Young Frankenstein' a Monster Riot," *New York Times*, December 16, 1974.

43. Quoted in Parish, *It's Good to Be the King*, 205.

44. Robert Ross, *Marty Feldman: The Biography of a Comedy Legend* (Titan, 2011), 220.

45. William K. Knoedelseder, Jr., and Ellen Farley, "Comics and Films: Laughing All the Way to the Bank," *Los Angeles Times*, May 28, 1978; "If Tanen Exits, Feldman Also; Comic Hates U's 'Committee,'" *Variety*, December 7, 1977.

46. McGilligan, *Funny Man*, 336–337, 345, 353–354. He was the first person ever to be featured twice for the magazine's intensive interview; see Darrach, "Playboy Interview."

47. Eichenbaum, *The Director Within*, 165.

48. McGilligan, *Funny Man*, 368–369.

49. Well, that single word of Marceau's aside. See Richard Corliss, "What's Funny at the Movies?" *Newsday*, January 22, 1978.

50. Siskel, "No Kidding."

51. For Brooks's longtime love and observation of Keaton, see his interview with Dan Lybarger in *The Keaton Chronicle*, Autumn 1997 (www.tipjar.com/dan/melbrooks.htm).

52. McGilligan, *Funny Man*, 375–377, 418–419.

53. See Paul Gardner, "Hyphenates Seek Unified Film Approach," *New York Times*, February 25, 1974.

54. "Notes on People," *New York Times*, September 21, 1977.
55. Darrach, "Playboy Interview."
56. McGilligan, *Funny Man*, 511.
57. Guy Flatley, "John Denver Spreads the Word About 'Oh, God!'" *New York Times*, October 7, 1977.
58. "Multi-Talented Larry Gelbart Is at Home with Films, Theater, and Television," *Baltimore Sun*, November 23, 1977.
59. "Will Set Record for Most Hats," *Hartford Courant*, September 4, 1977.
60. Tynan, "Frolics," 54; "S.F. Film Festival Lauds Mel Brooks for Laughs," *Los Angeles Times*, October 11, 1977.
61. McGilligan, *Funny Man*, 383. For similar mediocre reviews, see M. H. Gardner, "'High Anxiety' Parody Needs a Point," *Baltimore Sun*, February 5, 1978; Gene Siskel, "'Anxiety' Is Good but Not as Crazy as It Should Be," *Chicago Tribune*, February 3, 1978; Art Harris, "On Shrinks and Kinks," *Washington Post*, February 3, 1978; Joy Gould Boyum, "Predictable Spoof of Hitchcockiana," *Wall Street Journal*, December 28, 1977.
62. From Kenneth Tynan profile, in *Roger Ebert's Book of Film* (Norton, 1997), 513. *Gay News*, for their part, appreciated the shower scene, but were less sanguine about other stereotypical scenes in the film; see "High Anxiety," June 15, 1978.
63. In an interview for *High Anxiety*, Brooks explicitly said: "Homosexuals and Jews have contributed the most to my own life." See Donn Lee, "Brooks Goes Psycho," *Campaign* 31 (1978), 42.
64. Compare the comments Charles Champlin makes about "kidding on the square" in "Mel Brooks' 'High Anxiety,'" *Los Angeles Times*, December 23, 1977.
65. Yacowar, *Method in Madness*, 155; "Mel Brooks: What I Know Now," *AARP Magazine*, August–September 2015.
66. David Sterritt, "Two Zany Parodies from Mel Brooks Gang," *Christian Science Monitor*, January 16, 1978. See also Brooks, *All About Me!* 277–278, on the Brooks-Hitchcock relationship (and Hitchcock's comedic suggestion for the script).
67. In Joseph Gelmis, "If It's Anhedonic, It Must Be Allen," *Newsday*, April 17, 1977.

68. Quoted in McGilligan, *Funny Man*, 387.
69. From Maurice Zolotow, "Mel Brooks: King of Clowns," *Reader's Digest*, April 1978, 129.
70. Ken Kelley, "A Conversation with the Real Woody Allen (Or Someone Just Like Him)," *Rolling Stone*, July 1, 1976, 36.
71. Mel Gussow, "Brooks Puts a Spin on 'Vertigo,'" *New York Times*, December 23, 1977.
72. "Stallone, Streisand 1–2 As Box Office Draws," *Los Angeles Times*, December 9, 1977.
73. "Mel Brooks Meets Joseph Heller," *Washington Post*, March 11, 1979.

Chapter 4. Jews in Space, and Time

1. Marc Kristal, "Brooks's Bookshop," *Saturday Review*, July–August 1983, 25, 28; Holtzman, *Seesaw*, 255.
2. Daniel, *Anne Bancroft: A Life*, 228–233.
3. Also close(ish) to home, Brooksfilms produced the R-rated comedy sketch film *Loose Shoes*, which featured Buddy Hackett and Kinky Friedman among others (including Bill Murray's first appearance on film). One skit includes people farting in submarines. McGilligan, *Funny Man*, 391, 394, 404, 437–444; Brooks, *All About Me!* 325–327.
4. McGilligan, *Funny Man*, 398.
5. "Brooks's Bookshop," 26. *The Elephant Man* was developed concurrently with a well-received Broadway production based on the same historical material; litigation ensued. See, for example, "'Elephant Man' Not from B'Way Hit; Same Title," *Variety*, May 16, 1979; "'Elephant Man' Screen Rights Involve Complex Legalities," *Variety*, July 18, 1979; "'B'way Hit Sues on 'Elephant Man' Title by Brooks," *Variety*, August 15, 1979; "'Elephant' Legit, Film Producers Settle Legal Tiff Out of Court," *Variety*, July 2, 1980.
6. Tynan, "Frolics," 130; Jerry Parker, "A Work of Hysterical Fiction," *Newsday*, June 14, 1981.
7. See Brooks, "The World According to Mel Brooks," *New York Times*, June 7, 1981; for Cantor, see Parish, *It's Good to Be the King*, 237.

8. Brooks, "The World."

9. Aaron Gold, "Jaws II Production Delayed by Snafus," *Hartford Courant*, November 17, 1977. I have (mostly) silently corrected the paper's spelling of the word "Mishagrass."

10. See, for example, Jack Kroll, "Schlock Yocks," *Newsweek*, June 22, 1981; R. H. Gardner, "'History' Succeeds in Being Outrageous," *Baltimore Sun*, June 16, 1981; "History of the World," *Variety*, June 10, 1981; Sheila Benson, "Brooks' History: The Formula Turns Sour," *Los Angeles Times*, June 11, 1981; Gene Siskel, "Funny, Uneven, Blast from the Past," *Chicago Tribune*, June 12, 1981; Jay Scott, "Mel Brooks' History a Lesson in Recycling," *Globe and Mail*, June 13, 1981. Compare, though, Vincent Canby's thoughtful "In Defense of Bad Jokes," *New York Times*, July 5, 1981.

11. Aljean Harmetz, "Hollywood Is Joyous over Record Breaking Summer," *New York Times*, September 9, 1981.

12. See Gene Siskel, "Mel Brooks Is Funnier Than Ever, If He Does Say So Himself—and He Does," *Chicago Tribune*, February 27, 1983.

13. Gorov, "Mel Brooks."

14. Bosley Crowther, "The Screen," *New York Times*, March 7, 1942.

15. Ernst Lubitsch, "Mr. Lubitsch Takes the Floor for Rebuttal," *New York Times*, March 29, 1942. Compare Daniel, *Anne Bancroft: A Life*, 240–241.

16. Noël Coward took a similar approach in his acidly ironic wartime song "Let's Not Be Beastly to the Germans": "Let's be sweet to them/And day by day repeat to them/That sterilization simply isn't done." Compare John Mariani, "Let's Not Be Beastly to the Nazis," *Film Comment* 15:1 (January–February 1979), 49–53, which points out other wartime acts of ridicule ranging from Charlie Chaplin to Donald Duck's *Der Führer's Face*.

17. McGilligan, *Funny Man*, 446, 456; Brooks, *All About Me!* 335–336.

18. See, for example, his discussion of directing *The Producers* in Darrach, "Playboy Interview."

19. Tynan, "Frolics," 88.

20. Although, Hollywood being what it is, it ended with the friend suing for feeling cut out of the process: see Daniel, *Anne Bancroft: A Life*, 240.

21. Carol Burton, "Annie's Back and the Hoods Have Got Her," *Newsday*, November 24, 1974; see also Norma Lee Browning, "Party for Peggy, a Special Love-In," *Chicago Tribune*, November 25, 1974. Thomas Meehan, one of the writers on Bancroft's 1970 special, co-wrote *To Be or Not to Be*; Brooks, *All About Me!* 332–336.

22. See, for example, Steven Kurutz, "How Do You Solve a Problem Like 'Manhattan'?" *New York Times*, March 1, 2018.

23. Gorov, "Mel Brooks."

24. The fact that the movie's director, Alan Johnson—who'd choreographed the "Springtime for Hitler" sequence in *The Producers* and the Inquisition number in *History of the World*—was gay certainly seems a possible factor in the shift, although Brooks himself, in interviews, champions the change as an important and significant one. See Siskel, "Mel Brooks," and compare McGilligan, *Funny Man*, 448, 453, and Daniel, *Anne Bancroft: A Life*, 241–243.

25. McGilligan, *Funny Man*, 452.

26. Quoted in Parish, *It's Good to Be the King*, 244.

27. On how *Solarbabies* got made, see Brooks's interview on the podcast *How Did This Get Made?* (www.slashfilm.com/mel-brooks-interview, May 26, 2016), and Brooks, *All About Me!* 354–356.

28. See McGilligan, *Funny Man*, 470–471; Daniel, *Anne Bancroft: A Life*, 243–244; Parish, *It's Good to Be the King*, 248–249.

29. Goldstein, "Launch Pad."

30. McGilligan, *Funny Man*, 477.

31. Gene Siskel, "On the Next Frontier, Mel Brooks Aims His Fazers at the Stars for a Space-Epic Parody," *Chicago Tribune*, January 11, 1987; Patrick Goldstein, "Mel Brooks, Back on the Launch Pad," *New York Times*, March 8, 1987. It should be said, though, that if the genre wasn't one of Brooks's natural favorites, the plot was inspired by something closer to home: the classic 1934 comedy *It Happened One Night*. Brooks, *All About Me!* 361–362.

32. Compare McGilligan, *Funny Man*, 486ff. Although there were exceptions, such as a piece by Jack Matthews in the *Los Ange-*

les Times, "Higher Anxiety," August 4, 1991, which suggests a new level of social relevance and pathos not seen in Brooks's films since *The Twelve Chairs*.

33. See McGilligan, *Funny Man*, 365–367; Brooks, *All About Me!* 381–383.

34. See Steve Pond, "You Wash Up, I'll Save France," *Washington Post*, November 5, 1981; McGilligan, *Funny Man*, 496.

35. Alec Matthew Klein, "The Bagel Pops Up as Toast of the Town," *Baltimore Sun*, January 19, 1996.

36. Gene Siskel, "Parody Is Overcooked, so 'Kentucky Fried Movie' Doesn't Quite Pan Out," *Chicago Tribune*, October 4, 1977.

37. Although despite its name, it also parodied TV commercials and newscasts, too.

38. While simultaneously quoting and hilariously decontextualizing some dialogue verbatim from original source material. I'm grateful to Stuart Weinstock for suggesting this to me.

39. Chris Chase, "At the Movies," *New York Times*, July 10, 1981.

40. Robert P. Laurence, "'Nutt House' Wobbly but Worth a Try," *San Diego Union-Tribune*, September 20, 1989.

Epilogue

1. McGilligan, *Funny Man*, 485, 512.

2. See Symons, "Prolonged," 346–347.

3. Parish, *It's Good to Be the King*, 263–264.

4. McGilligan, *Funny Man*, 516; Brooks, "Springtime for the Music Man"; Whitmire, "Q&A: Mel Brooks." Stroman actually took over as director, at Brooks's insistence, after her husband Michael Ockrent, the original director, died of leukemia. Brooks, in a statement that encompassed two thousand years of a certain Jewish comic sensibility, told Stroman "she might cry all night but he'd keep her laughing all day." McGilligan, *Funny Man*, 520.

5. David Lefkowitz, "B'way's *Producers* Raises 50 Top Tickets to $480 Each," *Playbill.com*, October 26, 2001; Patricia O'Haire and Robert Dominguez, "$480 Seats Music to 'Producers,'" *New York Daily News*, October 27, 2001.

6. Blake Green, "Tony, Meet Mel," *Newsday*, June 4, 2001; Scott Vogel, "Mel Brooks Laughs His Way to Kennedy Center Honor," *Washington Post*, December 6, 2009.

7. Ben Brantley, "A Scam That'll Knock 'Em Dead," *New York Times*, April 20, 2001; *New York Review* quote in Alex Symons, "Mass-Market Comedy: How Mel Brooks Adapted *The Producers* for Broadway and Made a Billion Dollars, 2001–2007," *Journal of Adaptation in Film & Performance* 1:2 (2008): 139.

8. The play itself was domesticated from its earlier version. Compare Fermaglich, "Mel Brooks' *The Producers*," and Symons, "Mass-Market Comedy," 133–145, esp. 137.

9. Lynda Gorov, "Shtick Shift at 76: Mel Brooks Is Red-Hot," *Boston Globe*, June 15, 2003.

10. It was, however, removed for the movie version. See McGilligan, *Funny Man*, 522–523, 532.

11. Vogel, "Treasure."

12. See Steven Zeitschik, "He Keeps on Joking While Revisiting His Hits," *Los Angeles Times*, December 10, 2012.

13. Belinda Luscombe, "10 Questions," *Time*, December 3, 2012.

14. See my article, "Why Larry David's Holocaust Joke Was So Uncomfortable," *Atlantic.com*, November 7, 2017.

15. Yohana Desta, "Carl Reiner and Mel Brooks Had Comedy's Most Iconic Friendship," *Vanity Fair*, June 30, 2020.

16. Mal Vincent, "Mel Brooks Sang for Mal Vincent," *The Virginian-Pilot*, July 31, 2015; Robert Kahn, "It's Alive!" *Newsday*, November 4, 2007; Cindy Adams, "Monster Work of Art Is Never Really Done," January 22, 2008; Jeremy McCarter, "Come On, Feel the Noise," *New York*, November 19, 2007; Michael Riedel, "Monster Salary Cuts," *New York Post*, June 6, 2008.

17. Michael Schulman, "Mel Brooks Writes It All Down," *New Yorker*, November 28, 2021 (www.newyorker.com/culture/the-new-yorker-interview/mel-brooks-writes-it-all-down).

18. Frances Hardy, "The Producer," *Daily Mail*, December 26, 2005; Adam Sternbergh, "History of *The Producers*, Part III," *New York*, December 12, 2005. And Brooks wasn't far off in terms

of his joke: *Spaceballs: The Animated Series* ran for thirteen episodes in 2008.

19. For a record of some of the changes, compare Sara Stewart, "Shtick Shift: Bawdy 'Producers' Tamed for H'wood," *New York Post*, December 11, 2005.

20. Scott Vogel, "I Am a National Treasure," *Washington Post*, December 6, 2009. Brooks reveals in his memoir that he was originally offered the honor by the George W. Bush administration, but declined "because as a veteran I was very unhappy about Americans being sent to war in Iraq"; *All About Me!* 437.

21. President Barack Obama, The White House, Office of the Press Secretary, "Remarks by the President at Reception for Kennedy Center Honorees," December 6, 2009 (https://obamawhite house.archives.gov/the-press-office/remarks-president-reception -kennedy-center-honorees).

22. Brooks, *All About Me!* 222; Julie Hirschfeld Davis, "Presenting America's Newest Comedy Team: Mel Brooks and Obama," *New York Times*, September 22, 2016.

23. Tynan, "Frolics," 60.

ACKNOWLEDGMENTS

EVEN SMALLER BOOKS acquire large debts; and it's my pleasure to acknowledge them. The first thank you goes to Steve Zipperstein, who's been a supporter of my writing from the very beginning, ever since a conference breakfast over twenty (!) years ago. I'm honored he asked me to be part of this series, and delighted for the fierce intelligence he brings to his editorial duties, balanced—and no mean feat, this—with his fierce warmth and friendship.

Research assistance by Jane Luca and Anruo Bao was essential to getting this book done, and I thank them both for their tireless efforts; and I'm grateful, as always, to the staffs of the Department of Germanic Languages, the Institute for Israel and Jewish Studies, and the Center for American Studies for their support, especially Dana Kresel, Sherene Alexander, and Angela Darling.

My colleagues at Columbia are always a source of intellectual inspiration to me; in the writing of this book, I'm particularly thankful for conversations with Andy Delbanco, Elisabeth Ladenson, Jim Shapiro, and Casey Blake. Adam Lowenstein and Stuart Weinstock both read the manuscript and I'm grateful to them for their feedback and their suggestions; I'm also grateful to the anonymous readers at Yale University Press for their comments, and to Phillip King for his mighty funny edit—no, wait; that should read mighty, funny edit.

Dan Conaway, agent extraordinaire, was, as always, a font of good advice and counsel. He's the best, people.

A significant chunk of this book was written during a time when my immediate family was staying with parents and in-laws during the first months of the Covid-19 pandemic. I've always known how lucky I was in picking my parents, and my wife's parents: but the patience, hospitality, love, and care that Eddie and Cheryl Dauber and Bob and Sherry Pomerantz displayed under the most trying circumstances—including their children commandeering dining room tables as offices and their grandchildren using living rooms as construction paper depositories!—is extraordinary, and words are insufficient to thank them for it all. I'm also grateful to my siblings—Noah, Andrew, and Sara Dauber, and Rachel Pomerantz—for their support, love, and, in Rachel's case, some important perspective on *Robin Hood: Men in Tights*.

I'm a fan of funny movies and TV shows, to put it mildly, but if there are true sources of laughter in my life, they come from Eli, Ezra, and Talia. The jokes they tell, the games they play, the giggles they share, the smiles they give—I love them so.

And, in a book in no small part about performance and performers, the show-stopper: my wife Miri. What a lucky man I am, to have this beautiful, intelligent, and hilarious woman to share my life with. Over a decade ago, I dedicated a book published by this press to her, with lines from Shakespeare's sonnets. This time around, now that we finish each other's sentences a lot more frequently, maybe something a bit simpler, but no less heartfelt: WOW.

INDEX

Hawks, Howard, 107
Hefner, Hugh, 129
The Helen Morgan Story (TV play), 39
Heller, Joseph, 66, 70, 125
Henry, Buck, 74–75, 90
Hepburn, Katharine, 101
Herberg, Will, 49
Hercules (film), 84
High Anxiety (film), 2, 120–123, 132
Hiken, Nat, 33
History of the World, Part I (film), 117,
    128–132, 149, 157
Hitchcock, Alfred, 8, 120
Hitler, Adolf, 28, 132, 139, 154
Hoffman, Dustin, 88, 90, 107, 118
Hogan's Heroes (TV program), 76, 77
Holocaust (TV mini-series), 137
Home and Beauty (Maugham), 29
Hope, Bob, 44
Hopper, Hedda, 75
Horton, Edward Everett, 79
Hot Millions (film), 91
Hurt, John, 130

"I Get a Kick Out of You" (Porter),
    110
Ilf, Ilya, 92, 93
I Love Lucy (TV program), 33
Inside Danny Baker (Brooks), 66
Ionesco, Eugène, 80
Ishtar (film), 132
I Spy (TV program), 73
It Happened One Night (film), 186n31
It's in the Bag! (film), 92

Jacobson, Abbi, 158–159
Jacoby, Coleman, 33
Jaws (film), 127
The Jazz Singer (film), 8
Jenkins, Gordon, 59
Jessel, George, 50
Jewish Daily Forward, 7
Joe (film), 113
Johnson, Alan, 84, 186n24
Jones, James Earl, 101, 140
Jordan, Will, 76–77
Joyce, James, 83

Kael, Pauline, 87–88, 95
Kafka, Franz, 96
Kahn, Madeline, 2, 121, 122, 129, 150,
    159; in *Blazing Saddles*, 33, 113, 115
Kallen, Lucille, 19, 22, 28, 32
Kaminsky, Bernie (brother), 6
Kaminsky, Irving (brother), 6
Kaminsky, Lennie (brother), 6
Kaminsky, Max (father), 5
Kaminsky, Max (jazz musician), 11
Katz, Mickey, 49
Kaufman, George S., 42, 78
Kazin, Alfred, 5
Keaton, Buster, 8, 117
Keaton, Diane, 93
Keller, Helen, 59
Keller, Sheldon, 33, 34, 43–44
Kelly, Glen, 153
Kelly (musical), 65
Kennedy, John F., 71
The Kentucky Fried Movie (film), 148
Kilgallen, Dorothy, 75
King, David, 41–42
King Kong (film, 1933), 113
Kirby, Jack, 7
Kitt, Eartha, 36, 41
Kleinsinger, George, 35, 37
Korman, Harvey, 149, 180n17
Kovacs, Ernie, 33, 39–40
Kraft Music Hall (TV program), 59
Kroll, Alex, 75–76
Kubrick, Stanley, 91
Kundera, Milan, 96
Kutcher, Benjamin, 82

Ladd, Alan, Jr., 139
The Ladies' Man (film), 45
Lamarr, Hedy, 111
Landis, John, 148, 150
Lane, Nathan, 155
Langella, Frank, 93–94
Lapham, Lewis, 65
Laughton, Charles, 35
Lawrence, Peter, 36
Leachman, Cloris, 113–114, 115, 149
Lee, Peggy, 51
Lehrer, Tom, 58

JEWISH LIVES is a prizewinning series of interpretive biography designed to explore the many facets of Jewish identity. Individual volumes illuminate the imprint of Jewish figures upon literature, religion, philosophy, politics, cultural and economic life, and the arts and sciences. Subjects are paired with authors to elicit lively, deeply informed books that explore the range and depth of the Jewish experience from antiquity to the present.

Jewish Lives is a partnership of Yale University Press and the Leon D. Black Foundation. Ileene Smith is editorial director. Anita Shapira and Steven J. Zipperstein are series editors.

Solomon: The Lure of Wisdom, by Steven Weitzman
Steven Spielberg: A Life in Films, by Molly Haskell
Alfred Stieglitz: Taking Pictures, Making Painters, by Phyllis Rose
Barbra Streisand: Redefining Beauty, Femininity, and Power,
    by Neal Gabler
Leon Trotsky: A Revolutionary's Life, by Joshua Rubenstein
Warner Bros: The Making of an American Movie Studio,
    by David Thomson

FORTHCOMING TITLES INCLUDE:

Abraham, by Anthony Julius
Hannah Arendt, by Masha Gessen
Franz Boas, by Noga Arikha
Alfred Dreyfus, by Maurice Samuels
Anne Frank, by Ruth Franklin
Betty Friedan, by Rachel Shteir
George Gershwin, by Gary Giddins
Allen Ginsberg, by Ed Hirsch
Herod, by Martin Goodman
Jesus, by Jack Miles
Josephus, by Daniel Boyarin
Louis Kahn, by Gini Alhadeff
Mordecai Kaplan, by Jenna Weissman Joselit
Carole King, by Jane Eisner
Fiorello La Guardia, by Brenda Wineapple
Mahler, by Leon Botstein
Norman Mailer, by David Bromwich
Maimonides, by Alberto Manguel
Louis B. Mayer and Irving Thalberg, by Kenneth Turan
Golda Meir, by Deborah E. Lipstadt
Robert Oppenheimer, by David Rieff